THE BANKING SYSTEM IN THE COUNTRIES OF THE *EEC*
INSTITUTIONAL AND STRUCTURAL ASPECTS

The Banking System in the Countries of the EEC Institutional and Structural Aspects

Salvatore Mastropasqua

professor of comparative banking law
in the University of Cassino
Italy

1978
Sijthoff & Noordhoff International Publishers

ISBN 90 286 0518 5

Printed in the Netherlands.

CONTENTS

III LUXEMBURG

IV FRANCE

V GREAT BRITAIN

PREFACE

Although it was a Scot, Robert Burns, who reminded us that we had not the gift "to see ourselves as others see us" it is perhaps the British who, over the past century, have been the least inclined towards an objective approach. Well within living memory it was customary in foggy weather to say that the Continent was "cut off".

Thus, I pay tribute with some humility to the welcome assembly contained in this analysis of the banking controls and systems of the Common Market countries. The careful collection shows by contrast the absence of formality in the United Kingdom—the Bank of England in practice being like a Headmaster in a school—whose word is obeyed and whose source of authority is never questioned. The acceptance of a measure of formality will be less difficult because of the experience of the "lifeboat". This rescue of secondary banks showed the ability and authority of the Bank of England, although the event itself was a blemish arising from the absence of effective limitation on the institutions able to take deposits from the public and call themselves "bankers". They borrowed short and lent long.

To all concerned the work will be a help. The proposed EEC provisions for the harmonizing of banking inevitably adapt much of the regulation existing in the majority of countries of the Common Market. Thus especially does the English version of the work have value and appeal to all who will be faced with the new measure of uniformity. Particularly useful are the comments regarding the relationships between the banks and the Governments—the one area since the war where in the United Kingdom the absence of formality has been occasionally regretted.

Professor Mastropasqua is to be congratulated on his service to Europe and for his service to the English language readers.

F. R. Ryder

ACKNOWLEDGMENTS

This study was made possible by a NATO award. I would therefore like to thank firstly Mr. F. Welter, Administrator of Cultural Relations for the NATO. Furthermore, I wish to thank in particular Mr. H. Fournier, Formerly General Director of the Bank of France and director of the review "Banque"; Mr. P. W. van Romburgh, Chief of the Credit System Supervision Department, The Nederlandsche Bank; Mrs. M. P. Weides Schaeffer of the Board of Directors of the Commissionership for Control of the Banks, Luxemburg; Mr. P. Clarotti, Head of the Banking Department of the Commission of the European Communities; Mr. G. F. Calabresi, General Director of the Italian Banking Association; Mr. F. R. Ryder, Formerly Professor at the International Faculty for the Teaching of Comparative Law of Strasburg and International Legal Adviser, Midland Bank Ltd., London.

S. M.

INTRODUCTION

During recent years, all the industrialized countries have seen an economic recession of such an extent that it may be considered as the most acute since the second world war. Experts in political economy turn their attention to the causes of the crisis seeking to discover a cure for this affliction of the century, while the governments are in search of efficient means of intervention to emerge from the crisis which their country's economy is going through. The governments, for their part, meet the greatest difficulties in making forecasts or taking suitable measures, since the economic development of each country depends more and more on the international economic conjuncture, a fact which is illustrated by what the economists call "imported inflation".

One may find analogies between the crisis of the seventies and that of the thirties: in fact, apart from certain phenomena characteristic of the later crisis, for example "stagflation" and the paradoxical conjunction of unemployment and inflation in spite of Keynesian theories, both crises have entailed, and will continue to entail, important changes in the political and economic situation of certain countries.

Furthermore, faced with new demands which have arisen as a result of the evolution of the general economic context, the banking sector, the barometer of market economies, in spite of its proverbial attachment to tradition, is one of the economic sectors which is most ready to react and to adapt to transformations. Thus the banking sector forms a focus for the attention of economists and politicians and is besides the object of numerous structural reform projects, which bear witness to the continued effort to adapt legal forms to changing realities. It is in this spirit that, for example, the new Belgian banking law, the Dutch banking bill, the reform bills in England and the United States, as well as debates on the timeliness of credit reform in other countries, should be conceived.

It is still too early to estimate the extent of these reforms and structural changes, or to foresee the general course of the new model of organization in the years to come. This study, which examines the banking organization of the most industrialized countries of the Western world, aims, in the light of recent reforms and bills *in itinere*, to supply a first outline, an instrument which should be useful in giving a better understanding of the problems of comparative banking legislation, revealed by the economic crisis and monetary disorders of the seventies.

Moreover it goes without saying that, because of this interdependance of national economies, it becomes more and more useful to consider within an integrated and up to date context the structural and functional changes which have arisen in the different banking systems, which may have repercussions on the banking systems of other countries.

For this comparative examination, those countries of the European Economic Community which are most representative in the development of their banking sector have been chosen.

For each country, we will take into consideration, in outline, the general characteristics of the banking sector; the essential framework of current banking legislation; the bodies for direction and control of the sector (amongst which may be underlined here the pre-eminent role of the central banks, not only in their relation with the banking sector, but also in relation to the economy of each country); the different types of banking and credit institutions; the conditions for access to banking activity as well as supervision of the banking sector; the structure and organization of the Stock Exchange; lastly, the protection of banking secrecy.

In the last chapter, an attempt will be made to point out differences and analogies, as well as the most recent tendencies which have arisen in the banking world, and also to consider the problems of mixed banks, of generalization of credit, of banking internationalization and concentration, and the prospects for the evolution of the sector.

I HOLLAND

1. GENERAL CONSIDERATIONS ON THE DUTCH BANKING SYSTEM

The first Dutch banks were born in the course of the XVIIth century as exchange banks, and the Exchange Bank of Amsterdam (*De Amsterdamsche Wisselbank*), founded by the municipality of Amsterdam in 1609, is traditionally considered to be the most ancient Dutch Bank.[1]

During the XVIIIth century Amsterdam, thanks to its colonial power and to its highly favourable geographical position, was already one of the most important financial markets in the world. Towards the second half of the XIXth century the Dutch banks developed in the modern sense and in this period there arose, for example, *De Twentsche Bank* (1861), *De Rotterdamsche Bank* (1863) and *De Amsterdamsche Bank* (1871). Even now, in spite of decolonization, Holland still maintains a position of primary importance as an international financial centre. In fact, the Dutch banking system has a long tradition to its credit and, furthermore, profits from a rich experience particularly as regards foreign relations and international commercial transactions.

On the subject of banking legislation, the following must be mentioned:

(1) the Act of 23 April 1948 (S. I, 166) containing new provisions amending the statute of the central bank;

(2) the Act of 18 January 1952 (S. 35) concerning credit control;

(3) the Act of 21 June 1956 (S. 427) which modified the previous system of credit control;

(4) the Bill presented to Parliament on the 8th December 1970;
(5) the Reform Bill of 1975 submitted for the approval of Parliament and to which we shall return later.

Mention must also be made of the preparation of a new Civil Law which will replace the Civil Law of 1838 and which will also relate to commercial law.

Unlike other countries, such as Italy and Belgium, Dutch banking legislation has no banking law dating from the thirties. This is because in Holland there was no great banking crisis in the years from 1929 to 1933 such as those that involved most of the other European countries.

The legislative aspects of the Dutch banking system will be examined later, together with the organization of the central bank, banking institutions, and the powers of credit control, etc.; however, it may be noted here that Dutch banking legislation is characterized by its liberal spirit, its object being the defence of free competition, and that particular attention has always been paid to the problems of liquidity and solvency.

The following are amongst the most important innovations of the Dutch banking system in recent years: the growing tendency towards concentration of banking, the renewed expansion of the banks' foreign activities, the lengthening of the duration of credits granted to commerce and industry and, lastly, the tendency towards a decrease in sectional specialization.[2]

2. THE CENTRAL BANK

The Dutch central bank (*De Nederlandsche Bank n.v.*) was created in 1814 on the initiative of King William I.[3] Because of its origin as a private enterprise, the central bank is still organized under the form of a joint-stock company, but all the shares were nationalized in 1948.[4]

Since 1904 it has enjoyed the privilege *de facto* of issuing banknotes, while in 1948 it gained the privilege by law (art. 10 of the Banking Act of 1948). It has its headquarters in Amsterdam, a separate office in Rotterdam, as well as 15 branches and 39 agencies scattered about the rest of the country. Unlike in other countries, its capital belongs entirely to the state.

The direction of the bank is entrusted to two bodies:

(a) *the board of directors*, which consists of the President, the Secretary and from three to five Directors (art. 22 of the law of 1948), and whose members are all nominated by the Crown;

(b) the *Council of the Bank* composed of 17 members.

The central bank acts as a "bank of banks", i.e. as a lender in the last resort and as a supervisory body for the private banks. According to art. 9, paragraph I of the Banking Act of 1948, it has the duty of regulating the value of the Dutch monetary unit in the most favourable way for the prosperity and welfare of the country and, as far as possible, of stabilizing its value.

The central bank is therefore responsible for the monetary policy of the country, but maintains its autonomy with respect to the State; it also acts as an exchange office, i.e. as a supervisory body for currencies according to the terms of a regulation of currencies established by a decree of 10 October 1945. The Banking Act of 1948 reserves for the Minister of Finance the power to give instructions to the central bank in certain cases, but up to now this power has never been exercised.

3. CREDIT INSTITUTIONS: DEFINITIONS, DISTINCTIONS AND CLASSIFICATION

In Holland there is no legal definition of a bank, but it is understood to be characterized essentially by its role as an intermediary for credit, as well as in the creation of money.

A basic distinction between the credit institutions is made according as they are or are not subject to the central bank according to the 1956 Act on credit control.

(1) Amongst the banks which are subject to the supervision and control of the central bank are the commercial banks, the agricul-

tural credit banks, security credit institutions, general savings banks and central credit institutions.

(a)   The *commercial banks* generally carry out short term credit operations for commerce and industry. Since 1955 they have also been active in the field of medium term credit for which most of the other financial institutions showed little interest. At the same time, in recent years they have made a considerable effort to attract the savings of the public, which serve both to finance medium and long term credit and also to finance their operations on the financial market. Towards 1960 the commercial banks greatly increased the quantity of their foreign operations. Recently they have also increased their activity as "family banks", granting personal loans, loans to finance sales by instalments, cheques for payment. In this way they assume more and more the character of "universal" banks.[5] As may be seen, in Holland the model of the mixed bank has always remained in force and the commercial banks have always enjoyed the greatest liberty as far as their investments are concerned, although their resources are mostly composed of demand deposits. Furthermore they play an important role in the financial market.

Commercial banks can be set up in the form of joint-stock companies, or as general partnerships, or as limited partnerships or else in the form of an individual enterprise.

At present there are about 70 banks registered with the central bank; however this number tends to decrease as a result of the high level of concentration in banking.

All the Dutch commercial banks are members of the Dutch banking association (Nederlandse Bankiersvereniging) which, as the representative body for the sector, is consulted by the central bank when the latter is called on to give "general instructions" on the subject of banking. Furthermore, the Dutch Banking Association draws up the "general conditions" which regulate relations between the banks and their clients and which are applied as a contract of acceptance except in the case of an explicit wish to the contrary on the part of the banks or of their clients.

(b)   The *agricultural credit banks*, created after the example of the German *Raiffeisen* banks, are considered as being at the same time institutions for the creation of money and institutions for the gathering of savings. These banks, set up in the form of cooperative societies, are active above all in gathering funds in deposit and current accounts and in the assignment of agricultural credit. In the Dutch banking system they have a far greater importance than similar bodies in other countries. They carry out an activity of a local character, work on a cooperative basis and are affiliated to two institutions of agricultural credit (*Coöperatieve Centrale Raiffeisen Bank* and *Coöperatieve Centrale Boerenleenbank*), one at Utrecht and the other at Eindhoven. These operate as central bodies for the category and also as clearing funds for the banks which are affiliated to them. These central bodies are also empowered to give directives to the agricultural credit banks regarding their investments on the financial market. Recently the two institutions of agricultural credit have merged together.

(c) The *security credit institutions* (*effektenkredietinstellingen*) are all the bodies corporate, general partnerships and individual persons whose main activity is to function as intermediaries in stock-exchange operations. These institutions also gather funds in deposit and current account and grant credit to private clients.

(d) The *general savings banks*, according to the Act of 25 June 1956 which modified the system of credit control, are "all bodies corporate which devote themselves exclusively to the promotion of saving, and with that object accept monies on deposit on such terms that the possibility of calling the same is subject to limiting provisions, with the exception however of bodies corporate which are at the same time agricultural credit banks". At first they were not considered as being institutions for the creation of money, but during recent years their importance with respect to monetary policy has greatly increased and their field of activity has grown closer and closer to that of the commercial banks, as has also happened in other countries such as Belgium. The general savings banks, which invest their resources mainly on the financial market, must conform to the directives given them by the central bank. The majority of them are members of the Dutch Union of Savings

Banks (*De Nederlandsche Spaarbankbond*) which acts as a central body for the category of affiliated savings banks.

(e) The *central credit institutions* created by groups of banks are also considered as credit banks in so far as they themselves carry out banking activities.

The register of credit institutions held by the central bank is divided into four sections:

(i)   commercial banks and central credit institutions;
(ii)   agricultural credit banks;
(iii) security credit institutions;
(iv)   general savings banks.

Unlike in other countries, where operations relating to the market of stocks and shares are carried out exclusively by stock-brokers, on the Dutch stock-exchanges these operations are carried out both by stock-brokers and by the banks. In fact it is the latter who carry out the majority of negotiations on the stock-exchange.

In Holland there are no merchant banks, i.e. banks whose main activity is the acquisition of shares in non-banking enterprises. In fact the issuing of bonds and shares is carried out through the banks. In this way the banks' possession of non-banking shares is justified by the fact that they keep in their portfolio that part of the issue which was not placed at the moment of subscription. As against this, the central bank can exercise its control over the acquisition of banking shares by other banks. This is because in Holland the banks are the only institutions which must obtain prior authorization from the public authorities for any kind of merger. In fact, according to art. 13 of the 1956 Act, registered credit institutions may not enter into mergers with other enterprises or institutions, nor take a lasting participation in other credit institutions, whether registered or not, nor take over such institutions entirely, unless they have received prior authorization from the central bank. The central bank may, in fact, refuse this authorization if it considers that such an operation could have negative consequences for the credit system or else would be contrary to a sound banking policy. In this way the control of the central bank may be exercised not only on the banking mergers but also on the banks' shares in other banks.

Although in Holland the level of concentration is very high in banking, experience has shown that this has not brought about any decline in free competition, but has rather stimulated it. Furthermore, this process of concentration has carried out a selection, as a result of which the surviving banks have been invested with greater responsibilities at the national level.

(2) There is a certain number of credit institutions which are not subject to the control of the central bank. Amongst these a distinction must be made between the public or government-controlled institutions and the private ones.

(a) The public or government-controlled institutions:

(i) The Bank of the Dutch Municipalities (*Bank voor Nederlandsche Gemeenten*), half of whose capital is in the hands of the State and the other half is in the hands of the municipalities; it seeks to satisfy the financial needs of the municipalities and other public institutions, granting them medium and long term loans.

(ii) The Post Office Savings Bank *(Rijks Post Spaarbank)* which operates under the control of the State complying with directives issued by the public authorities, in close contact with the administration of the postal and telegraph services.

(iii) The Postal Orders Services (*Postchèque- en Girodienst*): there are two services, one of which is run by the State and the other by the municipality of Amsterdam.

(iv) The National Investment Bank (*Investerings Bank*), in which the State has a majority share, grants medium and long term credit to small and medium industries.

(vi) The Society for the Financing of Exports (*Export Financiering Maatschappij*).

It must be added that, because of Holland's liberal tradition, the public and semi-public sector of credit is relatively little developed, above all if it is compared with that of other European countries, as for instance Italy and France.

(b) The private institutions:

(i) banks specializing in personal loans;

(ii)   societies for the financing of sales by instalments, about 150 in number, the most important of which are affiliated to the large commercial banks and which are regulated by the general law on money loans of 28 January 1932 (S. 19), as well as by the law on the system of sales by instalments of 13 July 1961 (S. 218);
(iii)   the mortgage banks which grant mortgages to finance the purchase of real estate or ships;
(iv)   the land loan banks, of which there are a dozen, which are subject to a kind of self-regulation under the terms of an association of private law. Amongst other things, these rules give a maximum for the sums loaned out as well as excluding any activity apart from that of credit based on real property.

4. STRUCTURE AND ORGANIZATION OF THE STOCK-EXCHANGE

In Holland there are three stock-exchanges, in Amsterdam, Rotterdam and the Hague.

The structure of the Dutch stock-exchanges is quite particular in that they present elements in common with the private-oriented stock-exchanges (such as those of the United States and Great Britain) as well as with the public-oriented type (such as those of Germany and Austria): in fact, while on the one hand the Dutch stock-exchange is constituted in the form of a private association, on the other hand the credit banks play a pre-eminent role in them as intermediaries for stocks and shares.

All authority relative to the working of the stock-exchange belongs to a body derived from the Board of Directors which also carries out the functions of surveillance and organization of the stock-exchange market. The Board of Directors is composed of 15 members and a President.

Formally, control by the public authorities over the stock-exchange is within the competence of the Minister of Finance, but in reality these powers of control are exercised by the Board of Directors of the stock-exchange. Since 1914 only members of the stock-exchange can act as intermediaries for stocks and shares. Membership of the stock-exchange is conferred by the Board of Directors both on bodies corporate and on individual persons.

As already stated, the majority of members of the stock-exchange is made up of private bankers and of banks, which have their legal representatives in the stock-exchange.

5. ACCESS TO BANKING ACTIVITY AND THE NEW DUTCH BANKING LAW

As seen above, as a result of the law of 1955 on the supervision of credit, all firms and credit institutions, i.e. commercial banks, agricultural credit banks, security credit institutions and general savings banks are entered in one of the four registers held by the central bank; and only the institutions entered in the appropriate register are subject to the supervision of the latter. However the commercial banks and security credit institutions whose own funds do not reach a given amount fixed by the Minister of Finance are not entered in the register of credit institutions. Although entry in this register must be requested by the banks belonging to one of the categories provided for by the law, the central bank is nevertheless obliged to enter them, unless their own funds are below the minimum levels fixed by the Minister of Finance, in which case they can still carry out banking activities but without being entered in the aforesaid register.

The law does not indicate grounds for which registration may be refused. In case of refusal recourse may be made through administrative channels to the Crown, who, having heard the opinion of the Council of State, will decide the case.

According to the 1956 Banking Act no authorization is required for the exercise of banking activities and the formation of a new credit institution is not subject to any condition, save that of entry in the register held by the central bank in the case that its own funds (capital and reserves) exceed a certain amount. *This situation, justified by the traditional liberal principles of Dutch banking legislation, and, in particular, by the necessity of assuring free competition between firms, is in the process of transformation.*

In fact, the bill presently before parliament provides for the setting up of a system of authorization for access into the banking sector. In the first place, this bill defines as "credit institutions" legal entities, partnerships (*vennootschappen onder firma*), limited partnerships (*commanditaire vennootschappen*) which, and individuals who make it their business to obtain funds, withdrawable daily or at less than two years' notice, whether or not in the form of savings, and to grant credits and make investments on their own account; furthermore it establishes that no enterprise will be able to carry out banking activities without having first obtained authorization from the central bank, and therefore enterprises intending to carry out such activity will first have to apply to the central bank.

The latter must declare its decision within 90 days from the presentation of the application and a negative decision must be motivated. Refusal of authorization is foreseen in the following cases:
(a) if the enterprise requesting authorization does not respect certain conditions laid down by the same law;
(b) if the professional qualifications of one or more of the directors of the enterprise are not considered to be satisfactory by the central bank;
(c) if the central bank considers that the intentions or the respectability of the promoters or administrators of the enterprises are such as might compromise the security of the creditors.

The aforesaid authorization may be revoked if an enterprise which had obtained a licence ceases to exercise banking activities, if the enterprise fails to respect given conditions, or if the conditions required by the authorization are not met.

While previously the only denomination protected was that of "savings bank" the new law prohibits the use of the word "bank" or of its derivatives by any enterprise other than those registered. This prohibition does not apply to the central bank, nor to foreign central banks with agencies in the country, nor to the state postal savings bank nor, lastly, to foreign enterprises and credit institutions belonging to an EEC country and with branches in Holland.

6. SUPERVISION AND CONTROL OF THE BANKING SYSTEM

The bill revising the banking law takes into consideration not only the introduction of a generalized system of authorization for the exercise of banking activities and the protection of the denomination "bank", but also the central bank's powers of control which are considerably extended. Furthermore it contains provisions relating to the harmonization of banking legislation within the framework of the community, to the fixing of a certain number of coefficients, to an extension of the control already exercised by the central bank over credit institutions to other financial institutions, as well as the institution of a system of deposit insurance.

Therefore we will examine separately first the system of control provided for by the banking act of 1956 and then that set out in the bill of the new Dutch banking law.

(1) According to art. 10 of the 1956 Act the central bank, confronted with situations which might compromise the pursuit of the monetary policy for which it is responsible, is required to consult the representative associations of the registered credit institutions so as to lay down general directives valid for the banks belonging to the categories concerned, according to the practice based on the principle of a gentlemen's agreement.

If there is disagreement between the associations of the category and the central bank, the latter may make unilateral decisions; however, this case has never arisen since agreement has always been reached in the aforesaid consultations between the central bank and the associations of the category. This system allows the banks to carry out a form of self-discipline in the sector.

As for the control of liquidity and solvency, the central bank can also give directions on the running of registered credit institutions. If it ascertains that a given institution has not abided by these directions, it can send new and more detailed instructions requesting the credit institution concerned to comply with them within a given period. If even in this case the bank does not follow the instructions of the central bank, the latter may then, in the last resort, make the matter public. This measure, whose consequences may easily be imagined has never up to now been put into practice.

According to other provisions of the 1956 Act, the central bank may request any information from the registered credit institutions and the aforesaid institutions must submit annually to the central bank a balance sheet and an account of profits and losses.

It must be added that, in Holland, although the central bank according to art. 15 of the 1956 Act may arrange the inspection of the book-keeping of registered credit institutions, there is no system of control by bank auditors as there is for example in Belgium; however in recent years an ever greater number of banks have submitted their books to experts, thus carrying out a kind of self-control over their own book-keeping.

As for structural policy, i.e. control over the structures of the registered credit institutions, art. 13 of the 1956 Banking Act prohibits these institutions from proceeding—without prior authorization from the central bank—to any reduction in subscribed or deposited capital, to any acquisition of permanent shares in other credit institutions, to any merger with other enterprises or institutions and lastly to the adoption of any measure of financial reorganization.

In Holland a system of *obligatory reserves* has been in operation since 1952, made up mostly of ready money and Treasury bonds; on the basis of this system the central bank may fix *liquidity ratios* relative both to short term deposits (i.e. less than two years), to long term deposits, and lastly to savings deposits. These ratios may be modified every month according to the requirements of the country's monetary policy, in agreement with the representative associations of the banks. The legal foundation of this system, also called the system of indirect credit control, is to be found in art. 10 of the 1956 Banking Act.[6]

(2) As well as the introduction of a generalized system of authorization for access to the banking sector, the bill of the new banking

law considerably reinforces and extends the central bank's powers of control.

Previously, institutions which assigned credit using only funds collected on a long term basis did not enter into the legal definition of credit institutions, and were therefore not subject to the provisions of the 1956 Act on credit control. On this matter the government decided that—from the point of view of the protection of creditors—rather than taking into consideration for how long the funds were deposited, it was preferable to take as a basis the solidity of the financial institution. For this reason, section 30 of the new law provides for the possibility of extending the surveillance of the central bank to financial institutions which are not included amongst the credit institutions properly so-called since they collect funds on a long term basis. Naturally it will be possible to apply to these financial institutions, *mutatis mutandis*, the provisions of the banking law on control of credit institutions.

In fact, when this regulation has entered into force, the central bank will be able to carry out its own surveillance, not only over the credit institutions but also over all financial institutions operating on the capital market.

Furthermore, on the subject of structural policy, new cases are introduced in which it is necessary to seek approval from the government of central bank, which must grant a special "nulla osta" (*verklaring van geen bezwaar*). It has been specified in particular that prior authorization must be sought for any acquisition by the banks of shares in other enterprises or institutions when this exceeds the value of 5% of the capital. Authorization must also be sought by anybody in a position to exercise control, direct or indirect, in a credit institution, as for example when he disposes of more than a twentieth part of the votes in the general assembly of the bank.

There are also new provisions relating to the directions which the central bank can give to credit institutions on the conduct of their affairs so as to ensure their solvency and liquidity, as well as to the questions of fixing ratios.

Although the harmonization of banking legislation amongst the countries of the EEC is still far from being realized, the bill of the new Dutch banking law generally takes account of the consultations and agreements of the Community concerning the coordination of banking legislation at the level of the European Community, and also contains specific provisions conforming to the directives issued by the Council of the EEC on monetary policy.

Thus, for example, the provisions of section 43, which phohibits the use of the domination "bank" by non-registered enterprises, does admit an exception for banks which are already registered in another country of the EEC and which have branch offices in Holland. In fact this exception relates to the directive of the Council of the EEC dated 28/6/1973 concerning the suppression of restrictions on the freedom of establishment and freedom of activity in banking and finance. Similarly the provisions of section 22, paragraph 7 conform to the directive of the Council of the EEC dated 28/2/1974.

Furthermore the new law contains particular provisions concerning the failure of banks, which provide amongst other things for the intervention of the central bank in the court charged with the judicial procedure.

Lastly, in order to protect small savers, the new law ascribes to the government the power to impose on the banks a system of obligatory deposit insurance in case the representative associations of the banks do not themselves proceed to an insurance system on a contractual basis. It must be observed here that when this provision has entered into force, Holland will be the first country of the EEC to introduce a system of obligatory deposit insurance into its own legislation, similar to the system already existing in the United States where deposits are guaranteed by the F.D.I.C. (*Federal Deposit Insurance Corporation*) up to a sum of 10,000 dollars.

7. THE PROTECTION OF BANKING SECRECY

In Holland banking secrecy is not expressly provided for by the law. However art. 272 of the penal code is generally considered to be applicable to bankers. This states that "a person knowingly violating a secret which he knows he must observe by reason of his office, of his profession, or of a legal prescription, even if the office or profession in question has already ceased, is liable to a term of imprisonment of up to a year or else to a fine up to a maximum of 6,000 Florins."[7] The second sub-section of the same article lays down that "when such a crime is committed against a particular person, an action may be brought by the interested party". From this it may be deduced that the client can absolve the banker from the obligation of secrecy since in the case in question the secret is not absolute.

Although the credit institutions are amongst those which, according to the above-mentioned art. 272, are required to mantain professional secrecy, Dutch judges do not recognize the bankers' right to refuse to testify either in criminal trials or in civil suits, since the public interest in the pursual of justice must prevail over the particular interest of maintaining secrecy.

As for the protection of banking secrecy with respect to the revenue authorities, distinction must be made between the situation before and after the second world war. In fact, according to a decree issued in 1932 by the Minister of Finance, information was not to be gathered from banks or other similar institutions, the exercise of whose profession might be impaired if the revenue authorities made use of elements of information figuring in their administration; thus, at that time, banking secrecy with respect to the revenue authorities existed *de facto.*

This decree, which remained in force until 1945, was revoked after the war, as a result of which there is no longer any protection of banking secrecy with respect to the revenue authorities.

Lastly, as for banking secrecy with respect to the monetary authorities, it must be specified that according to art. 34 of the 1948 Banking Act, the President of the Council of the central bank may impose secrecy on the secretary and members of the council regarding everything they have learnt in the exercise of their office. Furthermore, art. 8, subsection V of the 1956 Banking Act lays down that no information concerning particular enterprises or credit institutions to be inscribed in the appropriate register may be published, such information being considered secret, while art. 14, subsection V of the same act lays down that no information concerning registered credit institutions, gathered by the central bank in the course of its duties, may be published, being considered secret except as provided for by the following art. 29.

NOTES

1. Van Dillen, "The Bank of Amsterdam", in *History of the principal public banks*, The Hague, 1934, p. 79f.; Bizaguet, "Les origines de la banque en Europe", in *Institutions et mécanismes bancaires dans les pays de la Communauté Economique Européenne*, I.D.E.F., pub. Dunod, Paris, 1969, p. 40.

2. For a more detailed description of the Dutch banking system cf. Repelius, "La banque aux Pays Bas", in *Institutions et mécanismes bancaires dans les pays de la CEE*, p. 537-622; Batenburg, Brower, Louman, "The Netherlands", in *Banking Systems*, Columbia University Press, New York, 1959; Wilson, "The Netherlands", in *Banking in Western Europe*, Oxford University Press, London, 1962; Karsten, "Banking in the Netherlands", in *Comparative Banking*, Waterlow and Sons, London, 1963; Bosman, "Das Bankwesen in den Niederlanden", in *Das Bankwesen in grösseren Europa*, Baden Baden, 1974.

3. De Jong, "The origin and the foundation of the Netherlands Bank", in *History of the principal public banks*; De Jong, "De Nederlandsche Bank", *Huit banques centrales européennes*, pub. P.U.F., Paris, 1963.

4. "Nationalization" should really be considered as the exclusion of foreign capital from enterprises destined to be nationalized in the sense of being handed over to national organizations (whether public or private). When understood in this sense, nationalization need not coincide with conversion to the public sector, which always consists of expropriation by the state or by public bodies of an entire sector of enterprises and implies the "deprivatization" and subjection to state monopoly of particular activities to the benefit of the state. However nationalization in the true sense may also coincide with conversion to the public sector, when in a given country there is no private capital sufficient to take over foreign shares, in which case the State will take over the burden. In current usage however the two concepts are considered to be identical. On nationalization in general cf. Chlepner, "Réflexions sur le problème

des nationalisations", in the *Revue de l'Institut de Sociologie*, no. 2 of 1949; Rivero, "Nationalisation", *Enc. Jur. Dalloz*, Paris, 1963; Katzarov, *Théorie de la nationalisation*, Neuchâtel, 1960.

5. Communautes Européennes, *La politique monétaire dans les pays de la CEE*, Luxemburg, 1972, p. 288.

6. De Nederlandsche Bank n.v., *Liquidity Requirement and Credit Control in the Netherlands*, March 1975; Id., "New Directives on Solvency and Liquidity", in *Quarterly Statistic*, September 1975, p. 74f.

7. Muller, "Le secret bancaire aux Pays-Bas", in *Le secret bancaire dans la CEE et en Suisse*, P.U.F., Paris, 1974, p. 99f.

II BELGIUM

1. GENERAL CONSIDERATIONS ON THE BELGIAN BANKING SYSTEM

The banking sector in Belgium developed simultaneously with the country's industry. Thus, when in the last century the textile, steel and chemical industries, mainly founded on the mineral resources of the country, reached a certain level of development, they found they needed the support of an adequate financial sector. This interdependance has always had considerable weight in the economic life of the country. Thus, during the economic depression of the thirties, the banks, which held a large number of shares in industrial and commercial societies, found themselves in a situation of growing non-liquidity, so that the economic crisis led to a crisis in the credit sector. This situation was the cause of the credit reform which entered into force on the Ist September 1935 and which put an end to mixed banks and separated financial societies from deposit banks.

In particular, the Act of 31 July 1934 ascribed to the government special powers so as to ensure the protection of savings and of banking activities, while royal decree of 28 August 1934 ratified the definitive division of mixed banks into financial societies and deposit banks.[1]

Later on, the 13th June 1935 saw the creation of the Institute for Rediscount and Guarantee (I.R.G.) set up to ensure in the short and medium term the mobilization of banking assets not rediscountable, because of their form or duration, with the central bank.

Lastly, with the enactment of royal decree no. 185 of 9 July

1935 a credit reform giving the banks a new legal statute and setting up the Banking Commission was launched.

This reform law, which was modified several times, chiefly by royal decree no. 67 of 30 November 1939 and by the Act of 3 May 1967 remained valid until the entry into force of the Act of 30 June 1975 "relating to the statute of banks, to private savings banks and to other financial intermediaries". Also known as the *loi mammouth*, this act has profoundly modified the legal statute of Belgian banks.

2. THE CENTRAL BANK

The National Bank of Belgium (*Banque Nationale de Belgique*) was created by the Act of 5 May 1850 on the initiative of the then Minister of Finance.[2] Originally it had three basic functions: the issuing of banknotes, credit activity proper and a cash service for the State.

Of these functions, that of direct dispenser of credit has by now lost all significance, while that of lender in the last resort has become more and more important, especially in the field of monetary policy since it has enabled the central bank to act directly on the liquidity of financial intermediaries. Originally it had the privilege, though not the monopoly, of issue, since Parliament could authorize private bankers and cooperative societies to issue bank-notes.

The central bank, set up in the form of a joint-stock company of which the State holds 50% of the capital, is controlled by the provisions of royal decree no. 29 of 24 August 1939, relating to the activities, the organization and the attributions of the National Bank, adopted in fulfilment of the law of I May 1939, which provisions have recently been modified by the Act of 11 April 1975. Another act of considerable importance is that of 28 December 1973 which ascribed to the National Bank, apart from the authority to fix its own interest rates, also the right of initiative in proposing measures of monetary policy. In particular this latter Act ascribed to the central bank the power to make "recommendations" to financial intermediaries and has increased the means of action traditionally at the disposal of the central bank so that all the banks, private savings banks and financial intermediaries of the public sector may be subject to the obligation: (1) to respect a given relation between the different elements of their assets and liabilities; (2) to respect given limits for certain elements of these assets and liabilities, limits which offer the central bank the possibility of setting up a form of quantitative credit control; (3) to place special deposits with the central bank which allow for the direct "sterilization" of the liquidity of financial intermediaries when this is judged to be excessive; (4) to respect the maximum interest rates applicable to the various categories of funds collected by the public.

The National Bank of Belgium has its central office in Brussels and furthermore sets up branches and agencies within the territory of the *Union Economique Belgo-Luxembourgeoise* (U.E.B.L.) where the need is felt and in agreement with the government concerned.

The governor of the National Bank is nominated by the King for a period of five years and presides over the board of directors, the governing council, the general council and the general assembly. The board of directors has a number of members varying between four and seven including the governor. All the members are nominated by the King for a period of six years on the proposal of the governing council, and the board devotes itself to the running of the Bank. The governing council, set up in 1926, deliberates on general questions relating to the bank, to the currency, to credit and to the economic development of the country; apart from the members of the board of directors, it also includes representatives from the world of industry, of commerce and of agriculture, from the trade-union organizations as well as from financial institutions of public interest. The general council is composed of the governor, the directors, the members of the governing council and the auditors; it devotes itself mainly to questions relating to the general organization of the Bank and to the remuneration of the governor and the directors. The college of auditors has between eight and ten members who are elected by the general assembly.

The National Bank also functions as State cashier, and in this respect it is subject to the control of the Court of Accounts.

Amongst the principal services of the National Bank, that of centre for risks should be underlined. This was set up on the basis of a voluntary agreement between the National Bank and the other banks in 1965 and its activity was officially recognized and extended by virtue of the royal decree of 9 October 1967. The centre for risks centralizes all information which the banks are required to communicate to the National Bank relating to granting, increase, reduction and suppression of credit above one million francs, as well as the use to which this credit is put.

3. MONETARY POLICY AND CENTRAL BODIES; THE BANKING COMMISSION AND BANK AUDITORS

The banks are subject to the authority of various bodies. The government determines general economic policy; amongst the various instruments of which it disposes to ensure its realization, there has been a tendency recently to attribute a determining role to monetary policy. Thus it is the government which defines the outlines, while it is up to the National Bank to propose concrete measures of monetary policy for the fulfilment of these general objectives, by means of the regulation of financial flows. Essentially therefore, the powers exercised by the National Bank in the field of monetary policy have the purpose of keeping banking activity within the framework of the economic and connected policies followed by the government.

It must however be underlined that monetary policy in Belgium takes on the character of "mutual consent" between financial intermediaries (banks, private savings banks and public credit institutions) and the authorities, for which there is a special committee presided over by the governor of the National Bank and including representatives of the Ministry of Finance and of the authorities controlling the financial sector.

For its part, the Treasury exercises an important influence, directly or indirectly, on the determination of credit rates, since it fixes interest rates for a substantial part of savings, to be exact that part made up of public loans.

Control of the banks is entrusted to the banking Commission, an "autonomous organization" according to royal decree no. 185 of 9 July 1935 which set it up, but in reality a body under government control. The Commission consists of a president and six members nominated by the King (and who may also be recalled by the King). A part of the Commission's working expenses is charged to the banks. The banking Commission is subject to the supervision of the Minister of Finance, in cases for which the organic decree of 1935 allows such interference; on the other hand, the existence of tutelage of a general kind has never been affirmed. The members of the Commission are required to maintain professional secrecy.[3]

The powers of the Commission were modified by the 1975 Act; in fact, the old art. 11 of royal decree no. 185 of 1935 allowed the Commission to determine periodically certain proportions between particular elements of the assets and particular elements of the liabilities which were to obtain in every bank. These so-called "structural ratios" were intended to maintain or favour the internal equilibrium of each bank; furthermore the same art. 11 allowed the Commission to determine ratios intended to favour the general equilibrium of the banking system, the financing of the State and the fulfilment of monetary policy. The latter coefficients, also called "macro-economic" are now within the competence of the National Bank following the new equilibrium established by the act of 28 December 1973 between the National Bank and the banking Commission.[4]

As for powers of control with respect to the banks, according to the organic decree of 1935 they were limited in practice to the supervision of the activities of bank auditors; however, following the modifications introduced by the 1975 Act, they have been considerably reinforced, especially with respect to interventions with single banks, as for example in the case of withdrawal of inscription or other exceptional measures.

The banking Commission also disposes of a prescribed power in the field of monetary policy, the exercise of which is subject to prior consultation with the National Bank, to the consent of the Minister of Finance, as well as to prior consultation with the Belgian Banking Association, as the representative body of the banking sector.

Although the banking Commission has powers of control over the banking sector as a whole, real day-to-day control is exercised by the "auditors" who are able to acquaint themselves in depth with the organization and functioning of each bank. The auditors are subject to the supervision of the banking Commission and are of a two-fold nature in that they carry out functions both of a private and of a public character.[5] However the latter functions have become more and more extensive so that they now prevail over those of a private nature.

The auditors must point out to the administrators and directors of the bank whose activities they supervise, any infraction; irregularity or omission which they may establish; furthermore they are required to pass on the same information to the banking Commission which may instruct them, whenever it considers it necessary, to present detailed reports. As a result of the 1975 Act it is now the banking Commission which fixes for each bank the number of auditors. The nomination of auditors is subject to the approval (granted for a period of three years and renewable only once) of the banking Commission, which determines the remuneration of the said auditors; and apart from this remuneration they may not receive any other emolument from the bank. Previously, on the other hand, the banks were free to choose auditors amongst those entered on the list held by the banking Commission. The list of auditors is revised periodically and they are subject to a strict discipline which in the case of a serious fault can lead to striking off from the list.

4. THE BANKS AND OTHER FINANCIAL INTERMEDIARIES

To understand the distinctions between the various types of bank existing in Belgium it is necessary to examine the situation before the reform of 1935. It has already been stated that the economic crisis of the thirties provoked serious difficulties in the banking sector, above all because of the banks' possession of shares in industrial companies. For this reason, so as to regain the confidence of savers, the 1935 Act of reform clearly separated holding companies from deposit banks thus putting an end to the so-called mixed banks. Thus for example, by virtue of this reform, the *Société Générale de Banque*, founded in 1822, kept for itself the role of holding company and created the *Banque de la Société Générale de Belgique* which took over its banking activities; the *Banque de Bruxelles*, founded in 1871, continued its holding activities under the name of *Société di Bruxelles pour la Finance et l'Industrie* (BRUFINA), while setting up a new and distinct company which took over the name of *Banque de Bruxelles* to continue its operations as a credit bank.[6]

By virtue of art. 3 of the royal decree no. 185 of 1935 only the enterprises entered in the list of banks set up by the banking Commission are entitled to make use of the terms "bank" or "banker", whether in the name of the firm, in the legal definition of the company's activity, or in their publicity. The name "bank" is reserved for those enterprises which usually collect deposits repayable on demand or within no more than two years, so as to use them on their own account in banking, credit or investment operations, with the exclusion of private savings banks which are controlled by special regulations.

Art. 14 of the royal decree no. 185 of 1935 provided for the prohibition, for banks set up in one of the forms provided for by art. 8, of the possession of stocks and shares of whatever kind.

However, from when the aforesaid law came into force, this prohibition has never been absolute, since four exceptions are provided for: (1) deposit banks could possess shares in other banks; (2) the aforesaid prohibition was not applicable to shares guaranteed by public bodies; (3) deposit banks could acquire in the short term shares intended for resale; (4) deposit banks could become owners of shares for the purpose of guaranteeing the payment of delayed credit for a period not exceeding two years.

It must be specified that the original text of art. 14 was noticeably modified by the Acts of 3 May 1967 and 30 June 1975. According to the 1967 Act it is possible to acquire shares without having recourse to subscription. Previously in fact, the banks could only acquire shares with a view to offering them for sale on the market within six months, while the 1967 Act laid down that the sale no longer had to be carried out in the form of a public offer and that the banks could hold shares for a period which on the basis of extensions granted by the banking Commission could be up to three years.

The Act of 30 June 1975 authorized the Commission to allow exceptions, in particular cases, to the prohibition against holding in whatever form stocks and shares in commercial companies. In this way, the Commission is able to evaluate cases in which according to the circumstances it is opportune or necessary to develop particular banking activities by means of a branch common to several institutions rather than within the framework of the bank itself.[7]

In applying this latter law, the Commission has authorized the holding of shares in companies whose activity is an extension in some sense of normal banking, as in the case of societies for the administration of common investment funds, companies for the issue of real estate certificates, leasing enterprises. Furthermore the Commission has used its powers of derogation to authorize a bank to hold, in expectation of their gradual elimination, shares acquired following the merger with a bank set up in the form of a personal company which as such was not subject to art. 14 of royal decree no. 185 of 1935.

Following the reform of 1934-35, capital belonging to banks set up as a result of the split between holding companies and deposit banks still stayed for the most part in the hands of the holding companies. Thus the problem of guaranteeing the independence of the banks could not be said to have been resolved. And so, so as to ensure the autonomy of banking, a series of "protocols" was drawn up in 1974 by the banking Commission and the three main banks of the country.[8]

By virtue of these protocols, the respective functions of the "board of directors" (responsible for the administration properly so-called of the bank) and of the "administrative council" (which has the duty, apart from the powers and attributions conferred on it directly by law or by statute, of defining the bank's general policy, delegating to the board of directors all or part of its administrative powers) have been distinguished and defined with precision. So as to avoid any legal uncertainty about the validity of the delegation of administrative powers to the board of directors as in the aforesaid protocols, the 1975 Act introduced a regulation authorizing the banks to provide, in their statutes, for a general delegation of such powers. Furthermore, the banking Commission has undertaken negotations with most of the banks with the intention of drawing up similar protocols.

By virtue of art. 5 of royal decree no. 185, modified by the 1975 Act "the banks are set up in the form of commercial companies". The new art. 5 has suppressed the old prohibition of the cooperative form, and at the same time has excluded the exercise of banking activities by individual persons, a form in any case long since vanished in Belgium.[9]

Whatever the legal form of the bank, the 1975 Act prescribes a minimum capital of 50,000,000 Belgian francs.

Nearly all the banks operating in Belgium are enrolled with the Belgian Banking Association. This association, as the representative body of the sector, is often consulted on the subject of monetary policy by the banking Commission and by other central bodies; furthermore its members participate in study commissions, in committees, etc.

The banks operating in Belgium are classified into four categories: banks with large-scale circulation, banks with medium-scale circulation, regional banks and specialized banks; the classification is laid down by the banking Commission.

Furthermore it is possible to distinguish between the banks under Belgian law and those under foreign law:[10] half-way through 1976 there were 64 banks under Belgian law and 22 banks under foreign law, forming a total of 86 banks entered in the register of banks held by the banking Commission with about 3,500 agencies.

The private savings banks, firms under the control of paragraph 1 of the Act of 10 June 1964 and holding companies also belong to the sector of financial intermediaries. In fact, in this sector, a "despecialization" allowing non-banking organizations to practise more and more the same type of operations as the banks, as well as the growing development of international movements of capital, have caused a tendency towards similarity between the statute of the banks and the statutes of the private savings banks and other financial intermediaries, so determining an extension of the instruments of monetary policy to all the categories of financial intermediaries.[11]

The *private savings banks*, previously controlled by royal decree no. 42 of 15 December 1934, modified by royal decree no. 11 of 18 April 1967 were not formerly subject to the organic control provided for by decree no. 185 of 1935; they were controlled by the Central Office for Small Savings, a public body set up by the Act of 7 December 1934 which in fact issued from the National Bank.

The private savings banks can collect deposits in various forms; however they devote themselves essentially to the collection of savings deposits, while most of their productive operations are in the field of mortgage credit and investment in savings funds.

Recently, the differences between the private savings banks and the banks have been growing less and less marked. For this reason, the first paragraph of the 1975 Act modified the legal statute and the control system for the savings banks, causing them to approach those of the banks. Thus, the 1975 Act provides for the subjection of the private savings banks to the control of the banking Commission and the suppression of the Central Office for Small Savings. More specifically, the royal decree of 23 January 1976 fixed the date of 30 April 1976 for the dissolution of the Central Office and the assumption of control over the private savings banks by the banking Commission.

The 1975 Act also laid down regulations for the minimum capital of private savings banks, fixing a total of 25,000,000 francs for those set up as joint-stock companies and a total of 10,000,000 francs for those set up in the form of cooperative societies; for control by auditors and for structural ratios; for exceptional measures to be taken by the banking Commission in particular cases; for the withdrawal of authorization to exercise activities; etc.

Lastly, the 1975 Act sets down regulations for the statute of about 800 Raiffeisen banks, which are confederated to and controlled by the Central Bank for Agricultural Credit.

The Act of 10 June 1964 relating to the collection of savings from the public laid down in art. 15 one of the fundamental rules of Belgian financial legislation: collection from the public (or advertisement with a view to such collection) of funds repayable on demand, after a given time, or by giving notice (including the discount of bills) is considered a crime except in the case when the funds are collected (or the advertisement is placed) by financial organizations subject to public control: these are the *enterprises controlled by paragraph 1 of the Act of 10 June 1964*.[12] Most of these enterprises devote themselves to collecting funds from the public with a view to granting loans and credits or to administering investment funds. The 1975 Act, in its third paragraph, assimilates the legal statute of such enterprises to the new legal statute of the banks: thus, the 1975 Act increased the minimum social capital or social fund of such enterprises to 25,000,000 francs (previously the minimum capital of such enterprises was fixed by royal decree no. 63 of 10 November 1967 at 5,000,000 francs); furthermore, the new Act provides, in certain situations, for the subjection of such enterprises to control by the banking Commission and by auditors and certain emergency measures, up to the withdrawal of registration.

The *holding companies*, whose main activity consists of participation in the capital of other companies in which they intend to exercise financial or technical control, are controlled by royal decree no. 64 of 10 November 1967 containing provisions for the statute of holding societies and for their association with economic programming. Art. 68 of the 1975 Act only modified the provisions of decree no. 64 on the point relating to control by auditors.

5. THE PUBLIC CREDIT SECTOR

Amongst the credit institutions, the public sector, which is fairly extensive in Belgium, must be considered.

The Institution for Rediscount and Guarantee, of which mention has already been made, is a State-controlled body set up on 13 June 1935 so as to ensure in the short and medium term the mobilization of banking assets not rediscountable with the National Bank. Its capital, to which the principal banks of the country subscribe, amounts to one billion francs. The institution, with a view to ensuring a better protection for savings and to face the risks of insolvency and illiquidity, can intervene in difficult cases, in conformity with the ends of public interest entrusted to it, so as to avert any situation which could compromise trust and the safety of deposits with a financial organization. Generally, this institution is presided over by a director of the National Bank.

The National Society for Credit to Industry was set up on 16 March 1919 to administer the National Bank's shares in commercial and industrial societies. 50% of its capital is held by the State and the other 50% by financial and banking groups.

The General Savings and Pensions Bank is a State-controlled body whose resources are made up essentially of savings deposits guaranteed by the State. As a public credit institution, the Bank administers the most important mass of savings deposits, in the legal meaning of the term, and has also issued, since 1968, "savings vouchers". Its resources are used mainly for loans for the construction of houses, for investment in public funds, and, to a lesser extent, for loans to industry and agriculture; it also contributes to the financing of exports and has recently begun to grant credit for hire-purchase, thus becoming a kind of large public bank with various activities. Paragraph VI of the 1975 Act introduced new provisions relating to the legal statute and control of the Bank, as well as of other public credit organizations.

The National Investment Society is a State-controlled body which specializes in taking over participations.

Other specialized State-controlled bodies grant medium and long term credit, generally financed by issuing their own money orders and bonds, to industry, agriculture, the private building sector, to craftsmen and local collectives. These are the *National Society for Lodgings, the National Bank for Professional Credit, the National Agricultural Credit Institution, the Central Office for Mortgage Credit, the National Society for Land Property* and *the Belgian Communal Credit.*

Lastly it should be added that the aforesaid public credit institutions are not subject to control by the banking Commission.

6. CONDITIONS FOR ACCESS TO BANKING ACTIVITY

As seen above, all enterprises, whether Belgian or foreign, which habitually collect deposits repayable on demand or within a period of less than two years, with the intention of using them on their own account in banking, credit or investment operations, must request entry in the register held by the banking Commission before beginning to carry out these activities.

When such a request for entry into the register of banks is presented, the banking Commission has the power to proceed to a thorough examination before announcing their decision; it may refuse registration and it may also withdraw it later on. The Commission makes enquiries into the identity of the promotors, their aims and intentions, the kind of activity which the new bank intends to carry out, into the means (in personal and in financial terms) and the organization which will be at its disposal. To this end, the Commission requests informative reports from experts who are particularly qualified. It declares itself in favour of the application only when it is convinced that the initiative is serious and well directed.[13]

It must be re-stated that the banks have to be set up in the form of commercial companies: this is justified by the need to separate the property of the bank from that of the partners, as well as the need for continuity of the banking enterprise.

Of the banks' directors, for their part, a certain respectability is expected and the law defines certain situations, incompatible with their functions, which they may not enter into.

Certain preliminary forms of control, for the commencement of activity, are also provided for other categories of financial intermediaries. In this respect, a certain terminological imprecision may be noted in the legislative texts, for the respective regulations speak of "registration" for the banks, of "authorization" for the private savings banks, and of "approval" for other financial intermediaries.[14]

7. CONTROL AND SUPERVISION OF THE BANKING SECTOR

Before the 1975 reform, which greatly changed the system of control of the banking sector, the regulations of Belgian banking legislation were full of gaps on this point. In fact, in the period preceeding the reform, the need to revise particular points of banking legislation had already been clearly felt and in particular its treatment of control of the financial sector. While under discussion in parliament, this need became more and more urgent following the revelation, in the autumn of 1974, of serious losses suffered by the *Banque de Bruxelles* in exchange operations, as well as following the initiation, in March 1975, of legal proceedings for the exportation of capital. And so the parliamentary debate on the problems of organizing public control over financial intermediaries provoked several amendments, on the initiative both of government and of parliament, of the reform project, tending in particular to reinforce control. This amongst other things explains the name "loi mammouth" by which the 1975 reform law is generally known. As far as regards, in particular, public control over financial intermediaries in the private sector, the new law noticeably widened the powers of the banking Commission. In the first place, the banking Commission has been given the power to seek clarifications and to order the communication of any information relating to the organization, the functioning, the accounting situation and operations of the banks and other financial intermediaries in the private sector.[15]

In the second place, the 1975 Act introduced important changes in the control system properly so-called. In fact, while under the regime of the 1935 legislation the banks were subject to the control of auditors and the latter to the control of the banking Commission, the new law affirms the principle that the banks, like all intermediaries of the financial sector are subject to the control of the banking Commission.[16] However the 1975 Act preserved the fundamental principles of the auditing system, emphasizing the function of the auditor as collaborator with the public control organizations; thus, for example, from now on the banking Commission establishes for each bank, both those set up under Belgian law and those set up under foreign law, the number of auditors, who may be withdrawn at any moment in the case of serious faults or of omission of their official duties; it also establishes the remuneration to be awarded to the auditors.

In the third place, the act extended the prescribed powers of the banking Commission regarding banking ratios, while laying down that regulations relating to these ratios are subject to prior approval by the Ministers of Finance and of Economic Affairs, and are to be adopted according to the opinion of the National Bank after consultation with the representative association of the banks. And so the banking Commission's constant practice of basing its actions on working in harmony with the institutions subject to its control has been consecrated by the text of the new banking law.[17]

Lastly, the 1975 Act ascribed to the banking Commission the power to impose suitable measures so as to overcome the crises to which banks are subject: "The new law introduces a system of intervention which is to operate in two phases. The first starts when the banking Commission ascertains that the functioning of a bank does not conform to the provisions in force, that its administration or financial situation do not offer sufficient guarantees for a good outcome to business undertaken, or else that the administrative organization or the international control present serious flaws. In this case the banking Commission gives instructions intended to restabilize the situation within a very short period of time. If this does not happen, the second phase begins, which entails several measures, adopted simultaneously or alternatively: the nomination of a special commission to give its written authorization for any decision of the bodies entrusted with the running of the bank; suspension of activities or at least of those in which irregularities were recognized, and, lastly, withdrawal of registration or of authorization".[18]

The control of the banking Commission is exercised not only over banking activities, but also over the organization of the banks. Thus for example mergers between banks must be authorized, on pain of annulment, by the banking Commission on whom therefore depends the degree of concentration in the banking sector. At first the banking Commission was fairly reluctant to admit such mergers, but it has since changed its attitude to view them with greater favour so as to stand up to the growing demands of international competition; at present therefore one may speak of a certain tendency towards concentration in the Belgian banking sector, exemplified by the merger, which took place in 1975, between the *Banque Lambert* and the *Banque de Bruxelles*.

In conclusion, although it is necessary to wait some time before being able to judge the efficacy of the new provisions of Belgian banking legislation, for now it may be affirmed that the recent reforms have allowed a considerable extension of the powers of the authorities with respect to the banking sector and a centralization of control over all the financial intermediaries of the private sector which has been entrusted to the banking Commission.

8. THE STOCK-EXCHANGE

The structure and organization of the stock-exchange in Belgium are modelled on those of the French stock-exchange, in that both are institutions under public law for which the brokerage of stocks and shares is reserved by the law exclusively for specialized intermediaries, i.e. the stock-brokers.

However there are some differences between the French and Belgian stock-exchanges, above all regarding the control system and the intervention of the public authorities. In fact, control over the Belgian stock-exchange is exercised by a government commissioner who has the duty of ensuring the observance of the laws and regulations in force, while a special committee has authority regarding the admission of stocks to the official quotation. It must be specified here that four stock-exchanges exist in Belgium, one of which, the Antwerp stock-exchange, founded in 1531, is the most ancient in Europe. The very name of "bourse" (stock-exchange) which was given for the first time to the Antwerp stock-exchange derives from the family name Van der Beurse of Bruges, who provided the usual meeting place for the merchants of *lettres de change.*

It must however be pointed out that the market of stocks and shares is relatively little developed, given that industry, in order to procure the capital it needs prefers to utilize holding companies and other public credit institutions (as for example the National Society for Credit to Industry) which generally issue a large number of bonds, thus collecting a considerable part of the country's usable savings.

9. BANKING SECRECY WITH RESPECT TO THE REVENUE AUTHORITIES

Banking secrecy in Belgium is not nowadays considered as professional secrecy in the true sense of the term, i.e. protected by penal law, in so far as at present there is no public investiture for the banking function, nor are the bankers, by definition, destined to receive the secrets of others, as happens for example with barristers, doctors and confessors;[19] in spite of this the foundation of banking secrecy rests on a long and scrupulous tradition of discretion.

With respect to banking secrecy, doctrine is divided into two camps: the first, made up mostly of criminal lawyers, accepts secrecy, while the second, made up mostly of commercial specialists denies it; the law, for its part, is not clear.

Before the reform of 1975 any investigation of banking operations was filtered through the bank auditors; at present, although the basic principles of the auditing system have remained unchanged, the growth in the powers of the authorities, and in particular those allowing the banking Commission to seek clarifications and to demand the communication of any information relating to banking operations, could lead to a weakening of the protection of banking secrecy.

It has already been seen that the banking Commission is required to maintain secrecy. Under the regime of the 1935 legislation the principle by which "the banking Commission does not devote itself to questions of a fiscal nature" was affirmed and also extended to auditors. The new law of 1975 introduced an exception to this principle, affirming that although the investigation of fiscal frauds is not amongst its prerogatives, the banking Commission is authorized to intervene whenever, through the supervision which it exercises over the running of banks, it ascertains that a bank, a private savings bank, or an enterprise under the control of paragraph I of the Act of 10 June 1964, "has put into practice a particular mechanism with the aim of favouring fiscal fraud by third parties". This regulation has given rise to contrasting interpretations of a legal nature in financial circles. So as to eliminate all uncertainty, the Minister of Finance set up a coordinating commission with the task of defining concretely the constituent elements of the putting into practice, by financial intermediaries, of "particular mechanisms" which should entail the intervention of the banking Commission. The coordinating commission has therefore set out to make a list of actions forbidden by art. 39, subsection II of royal decree no. 185, introduced into the Act of 30 June 1975.

It must anyway be underlined that the transfer of funds abroad by Belgian enterprises or citizens, in so far as such operations conform to the directives issued by the *Institut Belgo-Luxembourgeois du Change* (I.B.L.C.),[20] does not conflict, either with the letter or the spirit of any law, referring either to the depositor or to the financial institution carrying out these operations.[21]

NOTES

1. On the Belgian banking system cf. in general Chlepner, "Esquisse de l'évolution bancaire en Belgique", in *Revue de la Banque*, 1953, pp. 381f. and 513f; Johnson and Sayers, "Belgium", in *Banking in Western Europe*, Oxford University Press, London, 1962, p. 234f; Fierens, "Banking in Belgium", in *Comparative Banking*, Waterlow & Sons, London, 1963; Lambiotte, "An Outline of the Belgian Credit and Banking System", in *Fiftieth Anniversary Commemoration Lectures*, National Bank of Egypt, Cairo, 1965; Hoffmann, *Struktur des belgischen Banksystems*, Berlin, 1966; Geis, *Struktur des Bankwesen in Belgien*, Frankfurt am Main, 1969; Abraham and Simal, "Das Bankwesen in Belgien", in *Das Bankwesen in grösseren Europa*, Baden-Baden, 1974.

2. On the foundation and evolution of the National Bank of Belgium, cf. Van Elewyck, *La Banque Nationale de Belgique*, Falk, Brussels, 1913; Chlepner, *Belgian Banking and Banking Theory*, Washington, 1943; Kauch, *La Banque Nationale de Belgique*, Sobeli, Brusels, 1950; *Id.*, "Histoire de la Banque Nationale", in *Histoire des Finances Publiques en Belgique*, Vol. III, Brussels-Paris, 1955; De Voghel, "La Banque Nationale, Activité et Statuts", *ibid.*; De Brabandère and Pardon, "La banque en Belgique", in *Institutions et mécanismes bancaires dans les pays de la CEE*, Paris, 1969, p. 381f.

3. Cf. Bruyneel, "La loi du 30 Juin 1975, Mammouth, souris ou potpourri?", in *Journal des Tribunaux*, no. 4931, 22 November 1975, p. 652; *Id.*, "La Commission bancaire belge", in *Banque*, 1972, p. 13f., 125f. and 247f.

4. Cf. Bruyneel, *op. cit.*, p. 653.

5. Bruyneel, *op. cit.*, p. 653; Lempereur, "Le renforcement du statut légal des banques en Belgique", in *Banque*, 1976, p. 842.

6. Cf. Orsingher, *Les banques dans le monde*, Payot, Paris, 1964, p. 67.

7. Cf. the annual Report 1975-76 of the Belgian banking Commission, p. 33.

8. Cf. Demain, "L'autonomie de la fonction bancaire en Belgique", in *Reflets et perspectives de la vie économique*, I March 1976; Report of the banking Commission 1973-74, pp. 15-38. On this point cf. also Henrion, "La concertation et l'autonomie bancaire", in *Journal des Tribunaux*, 29 April 1972, no. 4783, p. 228f.

9. Cf. Bruyneel, *op. cit.*, p. 656.

10. Cf. Lempereur, "L'implantation en Belgique des banques étrangères", *Droit et pratique du commerce international*, 1975, p. 408.

11. Cf. Timmermans, *Les banques en Belgique*, Courtrai, 1969, p. 702f.

12. Cf. Bruyneel, *op. cit.*, p. 658.

13. Cf. the Report of the Belgian Banking Association, 1975, p. 61.

14. Cf. Bruyneel, *op. cit.*, p. 656.

15. It must here be specified that even before the 1975 reform the banking Commission, on the basis of agreements with the banks themselves, arranged for the supply of information even when not authorized by the 1935 legislation, so that on this point the new law did nothing but give a legal basis for practices which were already customary; cf. Godeaux, "L'encadrement de l'activité bancaire" in *La banque dans le monde de demain*, study conference of the Institut International Luxembourg, 1975, p. 90f.

16. Cf. Godeaux, *op. cit.*, p. 92; Lempereur, "Le renforcement du statut légal des banques en Belgique", p. 839.

17. Cf. Henrion, *op. cit.*; Godeaux, *op. cit.*

18. Cf. the annual Report of the banking Commission 1974-1975, p. 23.

19. Cf. Henrion, "Le secret bancaire en Belgique", in *Le secret bancaire dans la CEE et en Suisse*, Paris, 1974, p. 56f.

20. Furthermore it must be recalled that in the case of the Grand Duchy of Luxemburg, the dispositions relating to the exchange market are not operative, since Belgium and Luxemburg form part of the same monetary union which removes all obstacles to the free circulation of capital.

21. Annual Report 1975 of the Belgian Banking Association, p. 26.

III LUXEMBURG

1. GENERAL CONSIDERATIONS ON THE BANKING SYSTEM OF LUXEMBURG

Between the end of the XIXth century and the beginning of the XXth century Luxemburg passed from an agricultural phase to a very advanced industrial phase, thanks to the development of its steel industry. During the course of the last decade, the financial market of Luxemburg has seen an accelerated and spectacular development. The pre-eminent position held by the banking sector in Luxemburg bears no relation to its limited geographical extent, nor to the number of its inhabitants, but depends rather on a whole group of particularly favourable factors at the political and economic level. In fact, since the end of the second world war, a very liberal legislation has progressively attracted into the country both foreign banks and foreign investments.[1]

Thanks to its model banking organization, Luxemburg has overcome the monetary disorders which have arisen in the course of recent years without excessive difficulty, and indeed has acted as a refuge for foreign capital seeking a secure investment.

Unlike in other countries of western Europe, like Holland, England and France, up to now there has been no tendency towards banking concentration in Luxemburg.[2]

When talking about the banking legislation of Luxemburg, the first thing that must be considered is the creation of a special Commissionership for control of the banks (Grand-ducal decree of 17 October 1945). It is also necessary to mention the Grand-ducal decree of 19 June 1965 concerning banking and credit operations

as well as the issuing of stocks and shares; the ministerial regulation of 16 September 1971 setting up the Council for control over
the banks; the Grand-ducal decree of 22 December 1972 whose
aim was the control of investment funds; the Act of 2 June 1962
relating to conditions of entry and exercise of particular professions
and the Act of 26 August 1975 which has partly modified the Act
of 22 June 1962.

2. MONETARY POLICY AND CENTRAL BODIES;
THE COMMISSIONER FOR CONTROL OF THE BANKS

One of the chief characteristics of the banking system of Luxemburg is the lack of a central bank;[3] as far as the issue of bank-
notes is concerned, this is entrusted to the General Bank of the
State, a filiation of the Savings Bank, and to the International Bank
of Luxemburg (within the limit of 50,000,000 Luxemburg francs);
in any case, the currency issued by the General Bank represents
only about 5% of the currency in circulation while the rest is made
up of currency which is legal tender in Belgium.

At present, the monetary system of Luxemburg is based on a
monetary agreement between Belgium and Luxemburg dating from
1963, within the framework of the treaty setting up the *Union
Economique Belgo-Luxembourgeoise* (U.E.B.L.) while control over
exchange is entrusted to the *Institut Belgo-Luxembourgeois du
Change* (I.B.L.C.).

Since Luxemburg does not have a central bank, the country's
monetary policy is entrusted to the government which has delegated its practice to the Commissioner for control of the banks,
who becomes responsible *de facto* for carrying out the country's
monetary policy.

On the basis of art. 2 of the Grand-ducal decree of 17 October
1945, the Commissioner for control of the banks has the general
duty of ensuring the protection of savings and the ordered development of credit and of ensuring the observation of the laws, decrees and regulations relating to financial institutions and their
operations. Furthermore, the Commissioner has the power to pre-

pare, in agreement with the Minister of Finance, regulations concerning the budget and the accounting situation of the financial institutions; he holds the register of banks and the list of investment funds which have obtained "approval"; he also disposes of powers of inspection for the institutions subject to his supervision, with a view to checking not only the exactness of the balance-sheets and the periodic accounting situation but also any other information supplied to him. His powers of control also extend to banking and savings institutions (including the rural credit banks); to credit institutions other than the banks; to savings clubs administered by individual companies to investment funds set up or functioning according to the law of Luxemburg, as well as investment funds set up or functioning according to foreign legislation, when the shares of such funds are offered or sold publicy within the Grand Duchy; to trustee representatives.

The Commissioner for control of the banks is nominated by the Minister of Finance and has powers to nominate and to recall members of the auxiliary staff and to fix their retribution in agreement with the Minister of Finance. Periodically, or at least every three months, he presents to the Minister of Finance a detailed report on the general situation of the banks and the credit market.

The ministerial regulation of 16 September 1971 set up the Council for control of the banks, a body of a consultative nature, which has the duty of assisting the Commissioner in the exercise of his functions.

The Council for control of the banks is presided over by the Commissioner for control of the banks and has the duty of giving opinions on all questions subject to the examination of the Commissioner. The Council, by agreement with its president, may delegate the technical preparation of its opinions to specially designated committees of experts. The President of the Luxemburg Banking Association is also a member of the Council, and representatives of the banks are members of the committees of experts; in this way the banks are offered the possibility of participating in the running of the entire banking sector, thus accomplishing a kind of self-discipline within the sector. In the same spirit, the decisions

of the Commissioner are adopted, whenever possible, in agreement
with the credit institutions concerned.

3. BANKING ENTERPRISES AND CREDIT INSTITUTIONS: DEFINITIONS AND DISTINCTIONS

According to art. 1 of the Grand-ducal decree of 17 October 1945,
the authority of the Commissioner for control of the banks extends
to "banks, private savings enterprises, private enterprises for mortgage credit as well as all enterprises which collect deposits repayable on demand or in the short term, with the intention of using
them on their own account in credit or investment operations".

The Grand-ducal decree of 19 June 1965 makes a distinction
between *banking and savings enterprises* on the one hand and
credit institutions on the other. In particular, according to art. 1
of this decree "banking and savings enterprise, according to the
meaning of the present decree, must be understood to mean any
enterprise subject to the control of the Commissioner for control
of the banks, in conformity with the provisions of art. 1 of the
Grand-ducal decree of 17 October 1945 including the State Savings
Bank"; while, according to art. 12 of the same decree "credit institution, according to the meaning of the present decree, must be
understood to mean any individual person or body corporate other
than banking or savings enterprises provided for by art. 1, dedi-
cating itself habitually, as principal or secondary activity, to the
investment of capital". The credit institutions are also subject to
the provisions of the Grand-ducal decree of 17 October 1945 relating to banking control. Unlike the banking and savings enterprises, the credit institutions are not authorized to receive deposits
from third parties repayable on demand or at short notice to use
them on their own account in credit and investment operations.

In Luxemburg, all banks must be set up in the form of joint-
stock companies. Thus foreign banks installed in Luxemburg must
also be set up in the form of joint-stock companies. An exception
to this general rule, above all for historical reasons, is formed by

the rural banks which take the legal form of cooperative societies with variable capital and unlimited liability.

In Luxemburg there are not different kinds of banks; the only one to be distinguished from the others at the legal level is the State Savings Bank, which is a body under public law.

It could be affirmed that the banks of Luxemburg are of the "universal" kind, i.e. they are at the same time deposit banks and merchant banks.[4] However most of the activity of the Luxemburg banks consists of banking operations in the short term. As a matter of principle, the banks are not prohibited from holding shares in other industrial or commercial enterprises; all the same, this kind of activity is completely marginal. In any case, it is in this sector that the creation of a kind of national bank for shares is foreseen.[5]

A particularity of the financial market of Luxemburg is formed by the installation of several foreign banks, above all in recent years: at the end of 1974 there were nine Luxemburg banks and seventy-four foreign banks with a total of 518 agencies. In fact this phenomenon became evident above all from the end of the sixties with the appearance of the market in Euro-bonds, in Euro-dollars and Euro-credits, to such a point that the market of Luxemburg has become, together with that of London, one of the most important international financial markets.[6] Thus most of the business done by the banks of Luxemburg is carried out using foreign currencies. The importance of financial transactions with foreign countries is underlined by the fact that the value of exports and services supplied to foreign countries represents three quarters of the gross national product and this ratio has tended to increase in recent years.[7]

It has already been underlined that the development of the banking sector in Luxemburg was favoured by several factors, i.e. total liberty of exchange and circulation of capital; a strict but flexible system of banking control; an extremely liberal and not excessively analytical banking legislation; the absence of deductions at source from income deriving from bonds issued by non-residents; an extremely favourable fiscal regime for holding companies; a jealously guarded banking secrecy, etc.[8]

The banks with an office in Luxemburg can also take on the function of stock-brokers and carry out operations on the stock-exchange.[9] Most of the Luxemburg banks are members of the Association of Banks and Bankers of Luxemburg (A.B.B.L.), whose president, as already stated, is a member by right of the Council for control of the banks.

A quite special position is held by the Savings Bank, created by the Act of 12 February 1856 and having the nature of a body under public law. The Savings Bank performs various functions: unlike other banks, it devotes itself to medium and long term operations, above all on the internal market; furthermore, it has the duty, in agreement with the Minister of Finance and the Commissioner for control of the banks, of fixing interest rates; lastly, within the country, it has the function of clearing house. The Savings Bank also functions as General Bank of the State, in that it issues the currency of Luxemburg which, however, only represents 5% of the currency in circulation of the country.[10] The General Bank of the State, a filiation of the Savings Bank keeps separate books and enjoys a certain autonomy.

When talking of the financial market of Luxemburg, one must talk not only of the banking and savings institutions, but also of the *fonds d'investissement*[11] and the holding companies.[12]

As for the holding companies, which benefit, as already stated, from certain fiscal privileges, they can also proceed to financing operations. Their importance for financial activity in Luxemburg is witnessed by the progressive growth in the number of such companies and of their capital; thus, at the end of 1975, there were 4561 holding companies with a total capital of 179 billion Luxemburg francs.[13]

4. CONDITIONS FOR ADMISSION TO BANKING ACTIVITY

It would be a mistake to imagine that the liberal legislation in force in Luxemburg allows uncontrolled admission to banking activity.

In fact, to carry out banking activity in the Grand Duchy of Luxemburg, it is necessary to request personal and revokable authorization from the Minister for the middle classes, according to the Act of 2 June 1962, as modified by the Act of 26 August 1975, relating to conditions for the admission to and exercise of certain professions, as well as those for the setting up and administration of enterprises.

In particular, the Act of 26 August 1975 lays down that "authorizations relating to all professional activities in the financial sector will only be granted when they conform to the opinion of the Minister of Finance, who can, in particular, seek guarantees of a financial nature such as will not compromise the safety of the enterprise's creditors. A Grand-ducal regulation will determine, amongst other things, the minimum amount of social capital required for banking, savings and credit institutions".[14]

As regards the minimum capital, it is presently fixed, for banking and savings institutions, at 250 million Luxemburg francs, of which 150 million must be deposited on establishment; for credit institutions, it is fixed at ten million Luxemburg francs, all of which is to be deposited.

It must be pointed out that the bank Commissioner has the duty of investigating whether it is appropriate to grant authorization for admission to and exercise of banking activity. On the basis of his report, the Minister of Finance can give his opinion to the Minister for the middle classes, who is the only authority qualified to grant the aforesaid authorization. In this respect, account is taken, essentially, of the respectability and professional qualifications of the applicants,[15] since "guarantees of professional respectability are *de rigueur* in a field in which the risks of any abuse are particularly harmful".[16] The appraisal of respectability and professional qualifications has been extended, by interpretation, to the managers and the employees charged with the direction of a branch or agency.

In practice, it has been admitted that an assumption in favour of the application could result from a declaration by two banks already operating in Luxemburg for at least five years.

The aforesaid authorization is annulled whenever activity is suspended for at least one year, or has not been started within a period of two years from its concession. Since this authorization allows the bank to carry out its activities only in the main office, the opening of branches or agencies calls for the same formalities as those required for the opening of the main office. The authorization can be withdrawn for reasons that would have justified its refusal, or else when the beneficiary deliberately ignores the social and fiscal obligations imposed by this profession.

All decisions of the Minister relating to the concession, the refusal or the withdrawal of the aforesaid authorization may be contested by recourse to the Council of State within a period of one month from the notification of the contested decision.

According to art. 2 of the Grand-ducal decree of 19 June 1965 all banking and savings institutions, authorized to carry out banking activities on the basis of the Act of 2 June 1962, must be entered in the register held by the bank Commissioner. According to art. 3 of the same decree, only persons and institutions entered in the aforesaid register may make use of the names "bank", "banker", "savings bank" or any other name referring to the exercise of banking activity, so that this provision guarantees the protection of the term "bank".

5. THE SUPERVISION AND CONTROL OF THE BANKING SECTOR

The control system of the banking sector was perfected and reinforced in parallel with the development of banking activity in Luxemburg. The Grand-ducal decree of 17 October 1945 represents the basic text in which are contained the fundamental principles of the system of supervision and control of the banking sector. Later on, the powers of the bank Commissioner were widened firstly by the Grand-ducal decree of 19 June 1965 and secondly by the Grand-ducal decree of 22 December 1972, which had the object of controlling investment funds. It must, in any case, be underlined that the supervision and control of the Commissioner have always been exercised flexibly but effectively, according to the principle of moral persuasion.[17] In this way, the Commissioner's control has always been characterized by a spirit of collaboration between the Commissioner himself and banking circles.

The Commissioner, in the exercise of his statutory powers, has recently issued a regulation which provides for the periodic communication by banking institutions of a list of data on their activities. Apart from this, the Commissioner still has the power to ask banks for supplementary information, whatever the nature or type of the operations carried out.

One of the main innovations introduced by the Grand-ducal decree of 19 June 1965 was the fixing of banking ratios. In fact, according to art. 6 of this decree, the Commissioner can issue, by agreement with the Treasury Minister, regulations on the proportion which must hold between own assets and current liabilities for banking and savings institutions. This ratio, also called the "solvency ratio", can vary between the limits of 3 and 10%. However these rates can be modified by applying art. 8 of the same decree which lays down that the Commissioner can, on the agreement of the Treasure Minister, draw up special "conventions" whose object is the ordered development of credit and the liquidity policy of the banking system. When these conventions are drawn up together with the majority of banks, they can be made obligatory for all banks by means of a special administrative regulation. This system allows for the recourse to "conventions" between the Commissioner and the enterprises subject to his supervision in the form of gentlemen's agreements, so that one can also speak of a kind of "measured control".

According to art. 7 of the 1965 decree, the balance-sheet value of the total investments of a banking or savings institution made up of shares, of credits on branch offices, of land and ships as well as any other investment having the character of tied-up capital, may not exceed the amount of own funds as defined by art. 6 of the same decree; and in this case one talks of the "covering ratio for tied-up capital".

According to a recommendation of the Commissioner, short-

term assets (liquid assets, bank credits, and negotiable and rediscountable bill-portfolios) must come to at least 30% of current
liabilities (the so-called liquidity ratio).

In Luxemburg, unlike in other countries, as for example Belgium,
there is no system of auditing control over the property of banks,
independent of stock-holders of private trustee companies used to
this end; however, *de jure condendo,* it is considered that such a
practice could constitute an extra guarantee for creditors and
savers. This system of double control is presently in force only for
investment funds, on the basis of the Grand-ducal decree of 22 December 1972.

In Luxemburg there is no provision for forced liquidation procedures or controlled administration peculiar to the banking sector;
and so resource is had to the regulations in force for commercial
companies. However a bill, proposed by the bank Commissioner,
was presented to the government towards the end of 1974 so as to
introduce supervised administration into Luxemburg banking legislation as well as provisional administration and forced liquidation
of financial institutions subject to the control of the Commissioner;
this bill lays down, amongst other things, that the regime of supervised administration can be imposed following a justified request
not only by the bodies of the company, but also by a creditor or the
bank Commissioner who can also act officially. It is considered
that such a system could be more elastic and ensure a better protection of the interest of savers.

6. THE STOCK-EXCHANGE AND ITS ORGANIZATION

The Commercial Stock-Exchange of Luxemburg was set up by the
Act of 30 December 1927. Its organization, control over the operations carried out, the responsibility of brokers, its supervision and
every other measure relating to its functioning were the object of
an administrative regulation approved by the Grand-ducal decree
of 22 March 1928. According to art. 2 of this decree, the running,
administration and management of the stock-exchange are en-

trusted for a period of 99 years to the Joint-stock Company of the Luxemburg Stock-Exchange (*Société Anonyme de la Bourse de Luxembourg*), whose articles of association are approved by the Minister of Finance and 80% of whose capital is held by the State Savings Bank and by private banks, while 20% is held by private citizens.

The supervision over the functioning of the Commercial Stock-Exchange and the operations carried out there is entrusted to a government Commissioner who can inspect books, accounts, registers, or other bills and documents referring to stock-exchange transactions. The government Commissioner participates in the meetings of the administrative Council of the Stock-Exchange Company, with the duty of protecting the rights of the government and of opposing any resolution which he judges to be of such a nature as to violate the aforesaid rights, or which, in his opinion, are in contrast with the provisions of law or of the regulations. Only banks and stock-exchange operators resident in Luxemburg may act as stock-brokers, a title which is protected by the law.

The ever increasing importance of the stock-exchange is put into relief by the number of quotations, which rose from 119 in 1962 to 978 in 1975; its activity is marked by the prevalence of foreign securities which make up 87% of the total.[18] Furthermore, the Luxemburg market has become the principal stock-exchange centre for Euro-loans. In fact, the majority of Euro-loans are quoted by the Luxemburg Stock-Exchange, and the attraction exercised by this stock-exchange is explained, on the one hand by the speed with which a quotation may be obtained and, on the other hand, by the liberal and non-discriminatory control effected by the Stock-Exchange Company, as well as the relatively low level of expense needed to obtain a quotation. All the same, the Luxemburg Stock-Exchange is more a centre for quotation than for negotiation since most transactions occur outside the Stock-Exchange.

As for the mechanisms of negotiation and clearing of securities, it is necessary, lastly, to mention the presence of two bodies: Eurex (Eurex study syndicate) set up in 1973 on the initiative of the Luxemburg Stock-Exchange together with 69 banks from 14 countries; the joint-stock company Cedel (*Centrale de livraison des valeurs mobilières*), a neutral and independent body set up in 1970 by 72 founder banks from 12 countries. At present, about 640 financial institutions belong to this last organization.[19]

7. THE PROTECTION OF BANKING SECRECY

In the Luxemburg legal system, banking secrecy is not expressly provided for by any provision of law or of regulation; however, according to legal doctrine, the banker has an obligation and a right to professional secrecy, which obligation and right are not however, absolute and without variations.[20]

Banking secrecy is protected in different ways according to whether it is considered in relation to questions of an administrative or judicial nature or else to questions of a private nature.

As for questions of an administrative nature, it is necessary to distinguish between the positions of banking secrecy with respect to the monetary authorities and with respect to the revenue authorities. In the first case, banking secrecy may not be used against the bank Commissioner, who, according to art. 2 of the Grand-ducal decree of 17 October 1945, may inspect, in person or by means of delegates, the books, accounts, registers and any other bill and document in the possession of financial entreprises. According to art. 4 of the same decree, "without prejudice to the application of art. 29 of the penal code, as well as the obligations imposed on them by the present decree and with the exception of the case in which they are called to bear witness at court, the bank Commissioner and his delegates may not divulge facts with which they have become acquainted through the exercise of their duties". As for the delegates of the *Institut Belgo-Luxembourgeois du Change* (I.B. L.C.), who have powers of inspection for banks permitted to carry out exchange operations, they are liable to penal sanctions if they divulge any information learnt in the exercise of their duties.

In the second case, there are special provisions of law which provide for derogations of banking secrecy so as to ensure exact tax collection by the Luxemburg revenue authorities (see for example art. 33 of the Act of 8 July 1946; arts 17f and 30 of the Act of 28 January 1948; art. 8 of the Act of 7 June 1967). However it must be added that the international extradition treaties to which Luxemburg adheres do not consider tax infringements, so that no seizure or search of banks may be carried out in relation to fiscal frauds committed abroad.

As for questions of a judicial nature, there is some discussion as to the applicability to bankers of art. 458 of the penal code which imposes professional secrecy on "persons who hold, because of their state or their profession, secrets entrusted to them, with the exception of the case in which they are called to bear witness in court and the case in which the law obliges them to make such secrets known".[21] The problem is only posed at the judicial level, since, in practice, banking secrecy has never been put in doubt. More precisely, one may ask if the banker can be considered a "necessary confidant". This question has been answered in the affirmative, since the banker has received a true public investiture as the banking sector is intimately associated with the realization of the government's economic and social policy.[22] In addition, the obligation of secrecy is not identical for all professional sectors which are protected and the secrecy of the banker is relative and may therefore be dispensed with by consent of the interested party.[23]

As for commercial and civil suits in particular, a recent direction of the Supreme Court of Justice must be mentioned, according to which "persons holding as a result of their profession secrets which were entrusted to them because of their profession may, when they are called to witness in court, reveal such secrets but they may not be obliged to give evidence if they consider themselves bound in conscience to maintain secrecy".[24]

On the subject of penal justice, it is affirmed in general that the banker may not use his professional secrecy against the investigating authorities; however, to supply information to foreign legal authorities, the facts under incrimination have to be punishable equally in both countries.[25]

In any case it must be pointed out that the Luxemburg Banking

Association has always played an important role in the protection of banking secrecy, both in the banks' relations with the legal authorities and in those with government bodies.

Banking secrecy may also be opposed with regard to third parties, with the exception of certain hypotheses worked out by legal doctrine and by jurisprudence, as for example in the case of heirs, of certain partners, etc.

A particular feature of the banking system of Luxemburg, like that of Switzerland, which puts into relief the importance of banking secrecy, is the possibility of using so-called "coded accounts".[26] These accounts are current or deposit accounts of securities in which the name of the account-holder is substituted by a simple number so that a large number of bank employees will not get to know the identity of the account holder. Only a restricted number of people (for example the director or "Special Service" employees) knows the names of holders of coded accounts. These accounts are, in any case, considered equal to named accounts as regards the application of regulations of public law and of private law relating to the significance and extension of banking secrecy.

NOTES

1. Cf. Guill, "La banque au Luxembourg", *Institutions et mécanismes bancaires dans les pays de la CEE*; Rapport du Commissaire au contrôle des banques 1945-1975, Grand-Duché de Luxembourg; Meier, "Struktur des Bankwesen in Luxemburg", in *Strukturanalysen ausländischer Banksysteme*, Frankfurt am Main, 1971; Meier, "La structure du système bancaire au Grand-Duché de Luxembourg", in *Banque*, October 1976, p. 955; Deschenaux, "Das Bankwesen im Grössherzogtum Luxemburg", *Das Bankwesen im grösseren Europa*, Baden-Baden, 1974, p. 379.

2. In fact, in January 1977 the merger took place between the *Banque Internationale à Luxembourg* and the *Banque Lambert-Luxembourg* by absorption of the latter following a decision of an extraordinary general assembly of the two banks. In the spirit of both parties to the merger, the essential objective was the expansion of the field of activity of the

Banque Internationale especially at the international level, as well as the reinforcement of its means of action, this being seen in the perspective of development within a financial market which has acquired European dimensions in the last decade. It must also be mentioned that on the occasion of the integration, the *Banque Internationale* expressed its preference for a kind of administration of the Council of supervision-Directorate type. Thus, in expectation of the probable evolution of the legislation of commercial companies on this point, it has been decided to confer on the higher bodies of the bank a structure as similar as possible to that foreseen for this evolution.

3. In fact, there was a National Bank of the Grand Duchy of Luxemburg, created in 1873 and declared bankrupt in 1881; cf. Guill, *op. cit.*, p. 631.

4. Cf. Guill, *op. cit.*, p. 647; Meier, "La structure etc.", p. 956f.; Ruta, *Ordinamenti bancari dei paesi della CEE*, pub. Bancaria, Rome, 1971, p. 258.

5. Cf. Commission of the European Economic Community, *The participation of banks in other economic sectors*, Brussels, 1975, p. 25.

6. On the Eurobond market in general cf. Crochat, *Le Marché des eurodevises*, Paris, 1969; Einzig, *The Eurobond Market*, Macmillan, London, 1969.

7. Communautes Européennes, *La politique monétaire dans les pays de la CEE*, Luxembourg, 1972, p. 426.

8. Cf. Meier, "La structure etc.", p. 956.

9. In fact the only brokers presently permitted to operate on the Luxemburg Stock-Exchange are banks represented by their delegates; cf. Guill, *op. cit.*, p. 650.

10. On this subject, the *Banque Internationale à Luxembourg* should also be considered, as it still holds the right of issue, granted in 8 March 1856, within the limit of 50 million Luxemburg francs.

11. According to art. 1 of the Grand-Ducal decree of 22 December 1972, whose object was the control of investment funds, "the following are considered as investment funds ... common investment funds, investment companies and any other similar organization, whatever its legal form, in the sense that it carries out activities of collective investment of savings collected from the public through public or private offer of stock and shares or any security, whether negotiable or not, as well as any document representing such stocks or securities or conferring the right to their acquisition. All investment funds set up or functioning according to the Luxemburg law are subject to the supervision of the Commissioner for the control of the banks according to the regulations of the present decree. The same provision is to be applied to investment funds set up

or functioning according to foreign legislation when their securities are distributed, offered or sold in, or from, Luxemburg".

According to art. 4 of the same decree, "investment funds must be entered in a special register held by the Commissioner for the control of the banks. Entry and preservation in this register are subject to the condition that all the norms of law and of regulation regarding the activities and the functioning of investment funds, as well as the distribution, the placing and the sale of securities issued by the funds, are observed".

12. Cf. Delvaux, *Les sociétés holding au Grand-Duché de Luxembourg*, Sirey, Paris, 1969; Arendt, "Statut juridique des fonds communs de placement et des sociétés d'investissement au Grand-Duché de Luxembourg", in *Les organes collectifs de placement dans la perspective de la place financière de Luxembourg*, Luxembourg, 1970, p. 7f.

13. Cf. Meier, "La structure etc.", p. 967.

14. The Act of 26 August 1975 specifies later on that "no government authorization will be granted for the professions of securities broker and commission agent in the field of banking and credit activities or in the trading of stocks and shares. This limitation does not regard the activities of banking and savings enterprises, of credit institutions and stock-brokers, nor those in relation to the functions of stock-exchange operator amongst professional intermediaries of the financial sector".

15. With regard to these conditions, the Commissioner for the control of the banks and the government have always maintained that the administration of a banking enterprise which places in danger the property of depositors must be considered as lacking the legal requirements of professional qualification. And it is on this basis, sometimes together with a lack of the requirements of respectability, that some authorizations for the exercise of activities in the banking sector have been revoked in the past.

16. Cf. Council of State, 9 July 1971, question M.C.

17. Cf. Guill, *op cit.*, p. 647.

18. Cf. Meier, "La structure etc.", p. 965.

19. See the Report of the Commissioner for the control of the banks 1945-1975, p. 81f.

20. Cf. Schmit and Dondelinger, "Le secret bancaire en droit luxembourgeois", *Le secret bancaire dans la CEE et en Suisse*, P.U.F., Paris, 1974, p. 139.

21. Cf. for example Biewer and Weber, "Le secret professionel des banques en droit luxembourgeois", in *Feuilles de liaison de la conférence Saint-Yves*, Luxemburg, 1959, nos. 4 and 5, p. 99f.; Schmit and Dondelinger, *op. cit.*, p. 140f.

22. Cf. Dondelinger, "Réflections sur le secret bancaire", in *Cahiers*

des conférences du Centre d'Etudes Bancaires et Financières, Brussels, no. 212, June 1973, p. 15; Schmit and Dondelinger, *op. cit.*, p. 140f.

23. Cf. Schmit and Dondelinger, *op. cit.*, p. 147.

24. Cf. Higher Court of Justice (civil Cassation), 21 March 1957; *Id.* (civil appeal), 6 June 1961.

25. Cf. Schmit and Dondelinger, *op. cit.*, p. 149; Dondelinger, *op. cit.*, p. 17.

26. On banking secrecy and coded accounts in Switzerland, cf. Schonle, "Le secret bancaire en Suisse", in *Le secret bancaire dans la CEE et en Suisse*, p. 183; Aubert, *Le secret bancaire, la Suisse et les autres Etats*, Geneva, 1975; Zondervan, *Le secret bancaire suisse et sa légende*, Brussels, 1973.

IV FRANCE

1. FORMATION AND EVOLUTION OF THE FRENCH BANKING SYSTEM: HISTORICAL PRECEDENTS

Although the banking institutions in France have ancient traditions reaching back to the Renaissance, the full development of the French banking system took place at the beginning of the XIXth century, together with the appearance of the private bank, or *haute banque* as was generally called the small cosmopolitan group of merchant-bankers, above all Jews and Protestants, which constituted the banking *élite* and acted under the authority of the Bank of France, taking part in its direction thanks to their permanent presence in the Council of Regency.

To the "high bank" which was the bank of the rich and the nobility, were opposed first of all the local banks, the pawn-brokers which granted loans for pledges and other lesser institutions, and later the *grande banque*, i.e. the popular bank with many branches, which was concerned with small sums and small savers (without however offering the various services of the *haute banque*) and which was the nucleus for the formation of the great credit institutions in the modern sense.

Thanks as well to the industrial revolution and to the influence of the theories of Saint-Simon, the popular bank gradually caught up with and then overtook the high bank to a very considerable extent. Thus were born, towards the end of the XIXth century, commercial banks similar to the English joint-stock banks: the first bank created in the form of a joint-stock company was the *Comptoir National d'Escompte de la Ville de Paris* in 1848, which was followed by the *Crédit Industriel et Commercial* (1859), the *Crédit Lyonnais* (1863) and the *Société Générale* (1864). One may consider this evolution as being the crucial point in the development of the bank in the modern sense, and on it one may found the distinction between the *banques de dépôts* (or commercial banks) and the *banques d'affaires* (or merchant banks).[1]

2. THE LEGISLATIVE FRAME-WORK OF THE BANKING SYSTEM

The great crisis of the thirties also involved the banking system in France, although this crisis was less acute than in other European countries. However control of credit in France, which arrived with a certain delay in relation to the period of crisis, was imposed by the Acts of 13 June 1941 and 2 December 1945, which form the basis of French banking legislation.[2]

The law of 13 June 1941 did not introduce organic control but more simply traced the outlines of a future control system, limiting itself to giving a definition of banks and introducing a distinction between banks (which collect funds from the public repayable on demand or in less than two years) and financial institutions (which carry out credit and financial operations, without however collecting funds from the public). The same act also created the Permanent Committee for the Professional Organization of Banks and Financial Enterprises and Institutions, (substituted in 1945 by the National Credit Council) and the Commission for control of the banks, which had the task of supervising the application of banking legislation and which functioned both as a control body and as an administrative body for appeal against decisions of an individual nature first of the Permanent Committee and then of the National Credit Council.

The Act of 2 December 1945 "relating to the nationalization of the Bank of France and of the large banks and to the organization of credit", not only nationalized the Bank of France and the four large deposit banks, but also installed a system of direction and control of credit, completing the regulations of 1941, adopting the principle of the specialization of banks and creating the National Credit Council, which plays a double role, as a deliberative body and a consultative body, and which has substituted the Permanent Committee for Professional Organization of the Banks set up by the Act of 1941.[3] In particular the latter law introduced a distinction between *deposit banks* which collect deposits from the public repayable on demand or in less than two years, the *merchant banks*, whose main activity consists, apart from credit operations, in the assumption and administration of shares in existing enterprises or in enterprises under formation and which cannot invest in such operations funds repayable at sight or in less than two years, and the *medium and long term credit banks* whose main activity consists of the granting of credit for a period of not less than two years. These latter banks have aspects in common with the other two categories.

In application of art. 14 of the Act of 2 December 1945, decree no. 46-1246 of 28 May 1946 was issued, relating to the fundamental regulations for the functioning of the nationalized deposit banks and no. 46-1247 of 28 May 1946, relating to the fundamental regulations for the functioning of banks in the private sector. Some provisions of these decrees were repealed or modified by the decree of 25 January 1966.

It has already been said that the Acts of 13 June 1941 and 2 December 1945 constitute the fundamental texts of French banking legislation. However the principles established by these acts have undergone a series of adaptations and modifications. Thus, the Act of 2 December 1945 was modified, shortly after it came into force, by law no. 46-1071 of 17 May 1946. In fact, art. 5 of the Act of 2 December 1945 had introduced the principle of rigid banking specialization, which risked putting the whole category of merchant banks into difficulty; and so, art. 5 was modified, first by Act no. 46-1071 of 17 May 1946 and later by decree no. 66-81 of 22 January 1966. The latter decree suppressed the limitation to a period of two years for deposits managed by deposit banks and abolished all limitations to the collection of deposits by merchant banks.[4]

Thus, the principle of banking specialization, introduced by the 1945 Act, has undergone, above all in January 1966, important modifications which have had the effect of almost entirely eliminating the distinction between merchant banks and deposit banks; however the principle of specialization still holds for the long term financing sector, a sector which is the almost exclusive competence of public and semi-public credit institutions.

The decree of 23 December 1966 allowed deposit banks to hold shares up to a total not exceeding 20% (in place of the previous 10%) of the capital of non-banking enterprises, of financial institutions, of real estate companies or of societies providing services necessary for their administration.

The decree of 1 September 1967 raised from 75% to 100% of their resources the total amount of shares which deposit banks are authorized to acquire in industrial and commercial enterprises. As a result the existing differences between deposit banks and merchant banks became even less marked, and the duration of credits was lengthened according to the principle of "transformation" of demand and short term resources into means for long term financing.[5]

Furthermore, by decision of the National Credit Council on 10 January 1967 all previous limitations to the opening of banking agencies were annulled, thus giving back to the banks the full liberty which they had enjoyed in this field until the end of the second world war.

Since 1948 a liquidity ratio had been imposed on deposit banks and it was extended to merchant banks in 1966; the decree of 9 January 1967 officially set up the system of obligatory reserves.[6]

The evolution of the French banking system, following the reforms begun in 1966 on the basis of the decrees and the deliberations of the National Credit Council, has included a tendency towards the transformation of merchant banks into deposit banks, a marked tendency towards banking concentration, a rapid extension of the network of agencies, the orientation of the large deposit banks towards the system of universal bank and, lastly, the widening of their field of action.[7]

3. THE CENTRAL BANK

The institutional and structural frame-work of the French banking system is formed not only of banking and financial institutions properly so-called but also of bodies charged with the realization of credit policy, i.e. the Bank of France, the National Credit Council and the Commission for Control of the Banks.

The *Banque de France* was created by Napoleon in 1800.[8] Originally it was a private bank functioning as a discount and deposit bank, without any special privileges; from 1810 it was given the privilege of issue which became effective in 1848. The basic statutes of the Bank of France were issued in 1808 and completed and modified in 1836, while the Act of 2 December 1945 amongst other things nationalized the Bank of France, transferring its shares to the State. Although the latter act provided for the modification of the Bank's statutes before 28 February 1946, the 1936 statutes remained in force until 1973, when they were substituted by the Act of 3 January 1973 and the decree of 30 January 1973.

As for the management of the bank, it is entrusted to the governor, who is nominated by decree of the President of the Republic passed by the Council of Ministers, and is assisted by two vice-governors who carry out the duties delegated to them by the governor. The deliberating body of the Bank is the General Council, formed of the governor, the vice-governors and ten councillors: nine of these are nominated by a decree passed by the Council of Ministers and are chosen amongst persons of financial, monetary or economic competence while the tenth is elected by the personnel of the bank from amongst its members. Empowered by the decree of 30 January 1973 to set up committees including persons from outside the Bank, the General Council has set up at the Bank headquarters a Consultative Council composed of a number of members varying from 15 to 24 with the task of giving the governor opinions and informative reports on the situation and prospects of the various sectors of the economy; furthermore the General Council has set up "Councils" in the branches having at the local level the same assignments as the Consultative Council at the national level.

As for the Bank officials, who must be of French nationality, they are required to maintain professional secrecy.

The central office of the Bank is in Paris, Rue de la Vrillière, where it was installed in 1809 after taking over the old Hotel de Toulouse; its network of counters is composed of 234 branches and agencies.

The Bank of France, as affirmed by the statutes of 3 January 1973, "receves from the State the general task of supervising currency and credit"; the application of the State's monetary policy is therefore its responsibility. The Bank has the exclusive and unlimited privilege of issuing bank notes for all the metropolitan territory. There are five categories of productive operations for the issue of notes which are expressly indicated by the Bank's statutes: they are the operations on gold and currencies; discount operations; advances on public bills and stocks and shares; advances to the State; operations of acquisition and sale of public and private bills on the open market, also known as open market operations. Furthermore, the Bank of France also carries out a certain number of operations deriving from its qualities or resulting from various assignments amongst which should be remembered the central service for risks for credits which exceed a given amount; the central archive for unpaid cheques and the special service for the transference of funds between banks. Lastly it must be added that the Bank is also the administrative organ of the National Credit Council.

As for the organization and functioning of Clearing Houses, it must be mentioned that the Bank of France has set up Clearing Houses in all the markets where it has a branch, while in the capital there is the Clearing House for Paris Bankers *(Chambre de Compensation des Banquiers de Paris)*, set up in the form of an association controlled by the Act of 1901 and of which the Bank of France is only one of the members. Since 1969 the Bank of France has put into effect at the national level a clearing system based on a computer. The principle on which this system is based is the following: each bank taking part delivers every day to the central Bank a magnetic tape from its own computer on which are described all operations involving other banks. The central Bank's computer processes the tapes received from each bank and delivers to each a tape reproducing the operations in which it is involved. The banking institutions which have not automized their operations still have the possibility of taking part in the aforesaid clearing system by letting one of the participating banks represent them.[9]

No text provides for the direct intervention of the State in the running of the central bank's business and, although there are solid traditions of close collaboration between the government and the management of the Bank, formally it enjoys full independence.

The Bank of France, as an enterprise in which the State is the sole stock-holder, is obviously subject to the control of the latter. This control is exercised permanently by auditors and periodically by the Commission for the Auditing of the Accounts of Public Enterprises, which, however, according to the decree of 3 January 1966, "is not competent to examine and to judge the monetary policy and the credit policy followed by the bank".

4. THE NATIONAL CREDIT COUNCIL

The *Conseil National du Crédit* was created by the Act of 2 December 1945. It is composed of 45 members, most of whom are nominated by the Minister of Finance, and it is presided over by the latter. The vice-president is the governor of the Bank of France, who in most cases assumes the presidency *de facto*.

The National Credit Council constitutes a "little parliament",[10] amongst whose competences are those of making proposals, of giving opinions and of issuing regulations. In fact the Council may make recommendations and proposals to the Minister of Finance and to the Government on any question relating to the currency, savings or credit; furthermore it is consulted by the Minister of Finance on general credit policy, on the financial interventions of the State, and, more in general, on all questions which are submitted to the Minister of Finance.

With respect to the banks and financial institutions, the Council may adopt decisions of a general nature and decisions of an individual nature. Decisions of a general nature are addressed to the whole group of banking institutions subject to the authority of the Council, or rather to certain categories of such institutions and they regard in particular control over the remuneration of deposits (for example, in 1967 the Council forbade the remuneration of demand deposits, while it left free the conditions for the remuneration of non-demand deposits); control over the cost of credit which was concerned with minimum interest rates and was suppressed in 1966; control over the financing of hire purchase. Furthermore the Council introduced, entrusting its application to the Bank of France, the system of obligatory reserves and the retention coefficient for mobilizable assets, better known as "minimum portfolio of medium term credits or bonds".

On the individual level, the Council is authorized to make deliberations concerning entry in the register of banks and the registration of financial institutions, and also, as a disciplinary measure and on the initiative of the Commission for control of the banks, striking off from the register of banks and withdrawal of registration.

It is also authorized to order the closure of agencies and the limitation of the amount of deposits collected from the public, as well as to approve mergers, transfer of considerable parts of the capital of banks, transfer of considerable parts of their assets, etc. It must be added that these decisions of an individual nature are prepared by the "service of banks and financial institutions" of the Bank of France. Against all decisions of an individual nature taken by the Council, it is possible to appeal for annulment before the Commission for control of the banks.

5. THE COMMISSION FOR CONTROL OF THE BANKS

The *Commission de Contrôle des Banques* was created by the Act of 13 June 1941. Its assignments and its composition were modified and extended chiefly by the Act of 2 December 1945.

At present, the Commission for control of the banks is made up of five members: the president by right is the governor of the Bank of France, while other members are the president of the finance section of the Council of State, the director of the Treasury, a representative of the banks nominated by the Minister of Finance on the proposal of the Professional Association of the Banks and a representative of the personnel of the banks nominated by the Minister of Finance on the proposal of the trade-union organizations; in addition to these, there is a representative of the financial institutions when the work of the Commission is concerned with matters involving institutions of this type.

The Commission has the task of watching over the application of banking legislation; it therefore has powers of control, powers of regulation and disciplinary powers.

As for its powers of control, the Commission normally proceeds to the checking of documents and more precisely of accounting documents which the financial institutions are required to deliver periodically; furthermore it completes these controls with on the spot checks by inspectors of the Bank of France in institutions subject to its supervision.

As for its powers of regulation, they are exercised above all in the field of annual balance-sheets, of accounts of profits and losses and of periodical reports which the banks must deliver to the Commission, as well as on the subject of banking ratios. To this end the Commission has so far instituted the liquidity ratio, the ratio of use of stable resources and the ratio of distribution of non-rediscountable medium and long term credits.

As for its powers of discipline and jurisdiction, the Commission has the task of suppressing any violation of banking legislation and to this end it may inflict on banks and financial institutions disciplinary sanctions ranging from warning and censure to striking off from the list and withdrawal of registration. It is also authorized to make judgements on appeal on individual decisions taken by the National Credit Council. There is some discussion as to whether the Commission is a true body of administrative justice or more simply an administrative body of second order.[11] In any case, all

its decisions may be contested in the last resort before the Council
of State.

6. BANKS AND FINANCIAL INSTITUTIONS;
THE PROFESSIONAL ASSOCIATIONS

According to art. 1 of the Act of 13 June 1941, enterprises and
institutions are considered as being banks when, habitually and
professionally, they collect from the public, in the form of deposits
or in other forms, funds which they use on their own account in
discount operations, in credit operations or in financial operations.
Such enterprises and institutions must be entered in a special list
held by the National Credit Council and are subject to the supervision of the Commission for the control of the banks.

Although the Act of 2 December 1945 introduced a distinction
between deposit banks, merchant banks and medium and long term
credit banks (cf. above no. 2) it may be wondered if such a classification, before the modifications successively made to the banking
legislation, particularly following the reforms of 1966-67, which
provoked a considerable lessening of the differences existing between these categories and a certain approaching of their respective
statutes, still has a *raison d'être*. In fact the decree of 25 January
1966, specifying that deposit banks and merchant banks can collect
without differentiation demand deposits and deposits of whatever
duration, has considerably lessened the distinction between these
two categories. All the same, some differences still subsist on the
level of use of funds, since deposit banks are subject to more severe
restrictions regarding participation in other enterprises.

Amongst the deposit banks, a special position is occupied by the
nationalized banks, of which the State holds all the capital being
the sole stock-holder and which are subject to the same regulations
applicable to banks with private capital; they do not therefore
enjoy fiscal privileges nor do they receive financial contributions
from the State.

As for the merchant banks, a tendency must be recorded, above all since 1966, towards the transformation of such banks into deposit banks.

As for the medium and long term credit banks, which are anyway not very numerous, they may not collect deposits for a term of less than two years.

Furthermore, the law distinguishes the banks from the *financial institutions*: the latter carry out the same operations as the banks, i.e. discount operations, credit operations and financial operations; however, unlike the banks, they may not use their own funds for such purposes, so that the only criterion for distinction between the banks and the financial institutions lies in the origin of their resources.

As for their legal form, banks may be run either by an individual person or by a body corporate, but in the latter case they must have the form of general partnerships, of limited partnerships either simple or on a commanditary basis, or of joint-stock companies with fixed capital, excluding therefore the forms of limited companies and companies with variable capital, while financial institutions may be companies of any form.

As for minimum capital it is fixed for merchant banks at 20 million francs and at 10 million francs, according to whether or not they are set up in the form of joint-stock companies; for deposit banks it is fixed at 5 million francs (joint-stock companies) or at 2 million francs (personal companies and individual enterprises); for financial institutions the minimum capital required is less high.

As for the control of foreign banks, art. 15 of the Act of 13 June 1941 subjects them to the same regime as French banks. Previously, whatever the location of their main office, not only the branches of foreign banks were considered as being foreign banks but also French banks which, directly or indirectly, were controlled by individuals or bodies corporate of foreign nationality; however, following Act no. 75-601 of 10 July 1975 (which, in order to harmonize French banking legislation with a directive of the EEC, changed on various points the regulations applying to the nationality of the managers of banks and financial institutions) the criterion of control has ceased to be taken into consideration in the definition of foreign banks.

In fact, as a result of art. 7 of the Act of 13 June 1941, no one could carry on the profession of banker, nor, in consequence, direct or administer a financial institution, if he was not of French nationality, unless granted a derogation by the Minister for the Economy and Finance. These provisions, whose principles have been preserved, were however modified by the Act of 10 July 1975, in that citizens of member states of the European Economic Community were given the same status as French citizens, thus avoiding the necessity of derogation in favour of the former.

Previously foreign banks were entered in a special register set up by the National Credit Council and published in the Official Journal. However, the legislator, so as to eliminate all discrimination with regard to foreign banks, decided to do away with the special register of foreign banks and to enter all enterprises entitled to carry out banking activities in metropolitan France in a single register.

At the end of 1975, in all the territory of France there were 264 deposit banks, 27 merchant banks, and 58 medium and long term credit banks. Allowing for banks with a special legal statute, the total number of banking agencies presently amounts to about 18 thousand.

According to art. 24 of the Act of 13 June 1941, all banks, whether French or foreign, entered in the official register are required to belong to the Professional Association of Banks, which thus constitutes a kind of single and obligatory association for the category, with executive functions, representative functions for the associated enterprises, as well as consultative functions.[12] The Professional Association of Banks has the duty of passing on to its members decisions of the National Credit Council and the Commission for control of the banks, as well as the regulations concerning banks, and of ensuring their application; it gives its opinion when the National Credit Council intends to enter enterprises into the register or to strike them off and, furthermore, it is consulted whenever decisions of a general character have to be made which concern the whole group of banking operators; in fact it is the necessary intermediary body between the banks and the institutions of control.

As for the financial institutions, they are compulsorily grouped in the Professional Association of Financial Institutions, which carries out the same activities for the financial institutions as does the Professional Association of Banks for the banks.

7. INSCRIPTION OF BANKS AND REGISTRATION OF FINANCIAL INSTITUTIONS; OPENING OF BANKING AGENCIES

Since 1958, the National Credit Council has been the only body competent to examine applications for entry into the register of banks, to proceed to their classification and to examine applications for registration of financial institutions. Any application for inscription or registration must be presented through the professional association concerned, which will add its own opinion.

Before proceeding to inscription or to registration, the National Credit Council must make sure that the enterprise or individual making the application satisfies certain requirements relating to the abilities of the directors, the legal form and minimum capital. The decisions of the Council are prepared by the "service for banks and financial institutions" of the Bank of France. When the Council proceeds to the inscription of a bank, it expressly mentions in its decision the classification of the bank into one of the three categories provided for by the law.

According to art. 10 of the Act of 13 June 1941, the National Credit Council may refuse inscription in the register of banks (or registration as a financial institution) if the application does not seem justified by general or local economic necessities.

The council may also order the striking off from the register of banks or withdrawal of registration. Furthermore it may order the closure of agencies, limitation of the amount of deposits collected from the public, etc.; it is also competent to approve banking mergers, changes of some importance in possession of the capital of banks, etc.

It must also be mentioned that the Council may order the compulsory merger between particular banks when this measure is justified by general or local economic necessities (art. 34 of the Act of 13 June 1941).

As seen above, all decisions of an individual nature made by the Council may be contested before the Commission for control of the banks.

Following a decision of a general nature made by the National Credit Council on 10 January 1967, banks and financial institutions are no longer required to seek previous authorization for the opening of agencies. It must be specified that in this case the term "agency" means premises open to the public in which a bank may carry out the operations provided for and controlled by banking legislation, so that both large branch-offices and agencies with a large staff and also small offices working with few employees are considered as "agencies".

8. SUPERVISION OF THE BANKING SECTOR

The fundamental institutions to which supervision of banking activities in France is entrusted are the National Credit Council and the Commission for control of the banks.

As seen above, the Council is competent to make decisions both of a general nature and of an individual nature regarding banks and financial institutions and, in particular, to examine applications for entry in the register of banks; to proceed to their classifications; to order striking off of banks or withdrawal of registration for financial institutions; to order the closure of counters and the limitation of the amount of deposits collected from the public; to approve any banking merger as well as to impose it compulsorily when such a measure is justified by general or local economic necessities.

For its part, the Commission for control of the banks has the task of watching over the application of banking regulations. Thus, in order to allow the control of their administration, all banks are required to present to the Commission an annual balance sheet,

accounts of profits and losses, as well as quarterly reports conforming with specially prepared requirements, in terms fixed by the
Commission. The latter also has the power to grant derogations to
deposit banks intending to hold shares above the limit of 20% of
capital in enterprises other than banks, financial institutions, building societies or companies providing essential services for the exercise of their activities.

Regarding in particular the control of merchant banks set up in
the form of joint-stock companies and whose total balance sheet
together with obligations not included in the balance sheet exceeds
20 million francs, the Minister of Finance designates for them a
government Commissioner who attends all meetings of the administrative council, of committees set up within the council itself and
of the general assembly of stock-holders. The commissioner may
examine all the bank's documents and may veto any decision that
is in contrast with the national interest and which has been made
by the administrative council, by committees set up within the
council or by the general assembly.

On a more specifically technical level, the Bank of France also
has means of credit control at its disposal: this control is exercised
on the one hand through so-called indirect procedures which have
an influence on the liquidity situation of the banks and on the cost
of refinancing granted by the central bank and which are completed by the system of obligatory reserves and "minimum portfolio of medium term credits and bonds", which blocks mobilizable
assets in banks' portfolios; on the other hand there are procedures
for direct action on credit, with consist of the so-called "encadrement du crédit" (defined as a group of obligatory regulations de-
signed to limit the development of financial contributions), measures of direct supervision over certain kinds of credit and directives addressed to credit institutions inviting them to orient their
activities in the desired direction.

Lastly, mention must be made of the professional associations,
which have, respectively, consultative functions with regard to the
inscription of banks and the registration of financial institutions,
and also have disciplinary powers delegated by the Commission

for control of the banks; they thus have the function not only of necessary intermediaries between the banks (or the financial institutions) and the institutions of control, but they also allow the banks to operate a kind of self-discipline, however partial.

9. BANKS WITH SPECIAL LEGAL STATUTE

Apart from the banks entered in the register, it is necessary to consider the banks with special legal statute, which are not within the competence of the National Credit Council, although they carry out similar operations to those of the registered banks. These organizations are under the direct control of the public authorities and in particular of the Minister of Finance.

First of all, there are the *popular banks* specializing in credit for small and medium sized industrial and commercial enterprises. They carry out the same operations as deposit banks. The popular banks are all represented by the *Chambre Syndicale des Banques Populaires.*

Next there are the *agricultural credit banks* which are divided into banks affiliated to the National Agricultural Credit Bank and those not affiliated; the latter do not have the participation of the National Bank and are controlled by paragraph V of the rural code and by art. 5 of the ordinance of 16 October 1958. The agricultural credit banks also carry out long term operations, amongst which the issue of bonds and the concession of long term loans.

Furthermore there are the *medical insurance credit banks* which are grouped together in the National Confederation of Medical Insurance Credit.

Lastly, among the banks with special legal statute it is also necessary to consider the *societies for regional development* (S.D.R.), set up by the decree of 30 June 1955 which have essentially the task of participating, by means or shares in capital, in the financing of industrial enterprises in regions affected by unemployment or by insufficient economic development. They were set up with the participation of the large merchant banks and deposit banks and of the *Crédit National.*

10. THE PUBLIC AND SEMI-PUBLIC CREDIT SECTOR

It is difficult to make a precise distinction between the banks with special legal statute and the public and semi-public credit institutions. Thus one talks of credit institutions "under government control",[13] or else of institutions which are classed "at an intermediate level as linking bodies" between the banks properly so-called and the authorities charged with the realization of credit policy.[14]

The *Caisse des Dépôts et Consignations*, created in 1816, is a public body of an administrative nature.[15] It is directed by a Director General nominated by decree passed by the Council of Ministers, and it is controlled by a supervisory commission composed of members of parliament, of the Council of State, and of the Court of Accounts as well as the Governor of the Bank of France, the President of the Paris Chamber of Commerce and the Director of the Treasury. The Bank of Deposits originally had the task of receiving in consignment funds subject to litigation and legal securities; later on it was charged with the collection of funds from savings banks (both the National Savings Bank and ordinary savings banks), as well as with the running of the social security banks and most of the social welfare institutions. As against this, they grant medium and long term loans and make investments in stocks and shares, both of which activities are intended to finance local communities, the construction of habitations, and, to a lesser extent, investment in industrial sectors.

The sector of *savings banks* is divided into ordinary savings banks which are private institutions authorized to function on the basis of decrees issued in the form of regulations for public administration, and the National Savings Bank, founded in 1881 and subject to the authority of the Minister for the Postal and Telecommunications Services. The savings banks address most of their resources towards the public and semi-public sectors or towards

economic sectors which are judged to have priority. Although they
are still not considered as being on a par with the banks, the differences between the two categories are tending to diminish. In fact
there is a bill presently before parliament according to which savings
banks will be authorized to open current accounts for their depositors accompanied by a guarantee card. Once this bill is in force
it will entail a greater assimilation of the savings banks with the
banks with special legal statute.

The *postal order service*, run like the National Savings Bank by
the administration of the Postal and Telecommunications Service,
was set up by the act of 7 January 1918. It has no legal status, nor
financial autonomy; all the same it has become very extended and
ensures a cash service for its clients, thus facilitating the transfer
and collection of funds.

The French Bank for Foreign Trade *(Banque Française du Commerce Extérieur)* is a joint-stock company whose only share-holders
are the Bank of France, the National Agricultural Credit Bank, the
Bank of Deposits, the National Credit and the nationalized banks.
The president, the director general and the members of the administrative council are nominated by decree of the Minister of
Finance. Its object is to carry out all kinds of credit and exchange
operations on the condition that such operations relate to foreign
trade, and to facilitate the financing of all foreign trade operations
and of all kinds of medium and short term credit and of loans in
francs and foreign currencies, and to organize special procedures
to finance foreign trade for which it may receive advances from
the State.

The National State Markets Bank *(Caisse Nationale des Marchés de l'Etat)* was created in the form of a public enterprise with
legal status and financial autonomy by the Act of 19 August 1936,
to facilitate the financing of enterprises in possession of public
markets and the concession of professional credits. It may also intervene in favour of industrial, commercial and artisan enterprises.
It is run by an administrative council which includes representatives of the Bank of France, the Bank of Deposits, the Land
Credit Bank and some ministries; the administrative Council is

presided over by the president of the National Credit.

The National Credit (*Crédit National*) was set up in 1919 in the form of a joint-stock company to facilitate the repair of damages caused by the war and, for this purpose, it was given the task of carrying out special operations on behalf of the State, but, later on, it became the main medium and long term credit institution for industry. Its president-director general and the two directors who assist him are nominated by decree of the President of the Republic, on the proposal of the Minister of Finance.

The Land Credit Bank (*Crédit Foncier de France*) is a joint-stock company, founded in 1852, which has become a semi-public enterprise, under the supervision of the Minister of Finance and presided over by a governor nominated by decree, and which has progressively assumed several different roles amongst which, in particular, those of granting medium and long term loans to owners of real estate, with or without mortgage; of granting medium and long term loans known as "special loans" for the construction, extension and completion of real estate according to special laws; of organizing and supervising the mortgage credit market within the sector of credit for the construction and acquisition of habitations.

Both the Land Credit Bank and the National Credit procure most of their resources through the issue of long term bonds, and furthermore have at their disposal public funds intended for particular kinds of operations, as well as the proceeds of placing with banks medium term bonds negotiable on the market.

The Institution for Industrial Development (I.D.I.) was created in July 1970 to speed up the rate of growth of the nation's industry and, in particular, to facilitate the development of sectors considered to have priority, so as to give to national enterprises a European dimension.

In the French banking system, the public Treasury plays an ever more important role as financial intermediary, given that its activity, is not limited only to the administration properly so-called of the State's Finances. Although the Treasury is a public service of the State lacking a true legal status, it carries out functions both of financial administration and of a banking nature; in the latter case three attributions of the Treasury may be distinguished, i.e. that of deposit bank, that of medium and long term credit institution and that of merchant bank.[16]

In conclusion, the French banking system is based mainly on the large banks (*Crédit Lyonnais, Société Générale, Crédit industriel et Commercial, Banque de Paris et des Pays-Bas, Crédit Commercial de France, Banque Nationale de Paris*, this last being the result of a merger between the *Banque Nationale pour le Commerce et l'Industrie* and the *Comptoir Nationale d'Escompte de Paris*), whose activities extend over the whole national territory and which also play a dominant role in the international financial and stock-exchange markets; Besides these there is a large number of specialized institutions and smaller-sized banks whose activity is limited to one or two regions. If one also considers the credit institutions under government control and the public services and enterprises, it may be affirmed that enterprises belonging to the public sector in fact form the larger part of the French banking system, which however continues to be run in the spirit and according to the principles characteristic of private enterprises.[17]

11. STRUCTURE AND ORGANIZATION OF THE STOCK-EXCHANGE

Unlike the English and American stock-exchanges which are institutions of a private nature, the French stock-exchange constitutes a typical example of a stock-exchange organized in the form of a public institution, created by law and subject to the control of the public authorities.

The most ancient form of control of the French stock-exchange was the 1807 code of commerce which was later modified several times, in particular in 1942, in 1961 and in 1967.

Apart from the Paris stock-exchange which is by far the most important and which carries out the function of clearing house for the quotation of all stocks, there are also stock-exchanges in Bordeaux, Lille, Lyons, Marseilles, Toulouse, Nancy and Nantes.

As for persons authorized to carry out the activities of intermediary, the principle followed in France is that such activities may be carried out exclusively by specialized operators, i.e. stockbrokers, who are represented at the national level by the Company of Stock-brokers.

Control over the stock-exchange is exercised by the Minister of Finance and, since 1967, by the Commission for stock-exchange Operations (C.O.B.), which is a specialized public institution operating as a permanent body for the control of the Stock-Exchange.

The Commission for Stock-Exchange Operations is composed of five members, four of whom are appointed by the Minister of Finance, while the president is nominated by decree by the Council of Ministers. Two of the four members appointed by the Minister of Finance must be chosen amongst representatives of the banking and stock-exchange worlds. A Treasury official also participates in the meetings of the Commission in the capacity of government commissioner.

As for the admission of stocks and shares to quotation, it is within the competence of the aforesaid Commission, which must however seek the opinion of the Company of Stock-brokers.

The main characteristics of the French stock-exchange consist not only of the existence of a public body (the C.O.B.) which does not form part of the public administration properly so-called, but also in the existence of institutional forms of association for the exercise of activities of intermediation of stock-exchange operations.

12. BANKING SECRECY

In the French legal system, although there are provisions relating to professional secrecy, none of these refers expressly to banking secrecy.

However it is necessary to consider art. 378 of the penal code according to which "doctors, surgeons and other health officers, as well as chemists, obstetricians, and any other person who, by reason of status or profession, or as a result of temporary or permanent functions, is entrusted with secrets, and who, except in the case where the law obliges them or authorizes them to do so, reveals such secrets, may be punished with imprisonment from one to six months or with a fine from 500 to 3,000 francs".

However it has to be established whether bankers are amongst "all other persons entrusted with secrets by reason of status or profession". Certainly the public interest is at the basis of this provision of a penal nature and it cannot be doubted that, above all nowadays, the banker has become a necessary confidant; therefore the banker must be included amongst those whose profession demands the confidence of the public. However the intensity of secrecy is not the same in all the professional sectors which are protected, so that, whereas the secrecy of doctors, barristers and confessors is traditionally considered as absolute, other kinds of secrecy, like that of the banker, are relative and may thus be waived with the consent of the interested party.[18]

Some sentences of tribunals have considered art. 378 of the penal code as being applicable to bankers; however the Court of Cassation has still not pronounced a decision on this question.

In any case, there are exceptions to the principle of banking secrecy, and particularly in the case where the Commission for the control of the banks, according to art. 17 of the Act of 13 June 1941, asks for clarifications from inscribed banks or registered financial institutions, as also in the case where, above a given amount, the banks are required to declare credits granted to their clients to the central service for risks of the Bank of France. This amount is presently fixed at 200 thousand francs for the total of all credits granted to the same beneficiary by each bank, while limits varying between 5,000 and 50,000 francs are applied to the social security organizations.

It must however be specified that, above all since 1945, the idea that banking secrecy may not be used against the revenue administration has been strengthened, so that revenue agents may have access to all banking documents concerning contributors. Naturally the powers of the revenue authorities must be exercised within the limits laid down by the regulations of law, and in particular by arts. 1991 and 2002 of the C.G.I.

NOTES

1. Cf. Bigo, *Les banques françaises au cours du XIXème siècle*, pub. Sirey, Paris 1947; Germain-Martin, "France", in *Banking Systems*, Columbia University Press, 1959, p. 225f.; *Id.*, *Histoire et structure des institutions bancaires*, pub. Les Cours de Droit, Paris, 1964; Gille, *La banque et le crédit en France de 1815 à 1848*; Presses Universitaires de France, Paris, 1959; Bizaguet, "Banque et développement au XIXème siècle", in *Les banques de développement dans le monde*, Dunod, Paris, 1964, p. 49f.; *Id.*, "Les origines de la banque en Europe", in *Institutions et mécanismes bancaires dans les pays de la CEE*, Dunod, Paris, 1969, p. 59; Bogaert, *Les origines antiques de la banque de dépôt*, pub. Sijthoff, Leiden, 1966.

2. On the banking legislation of 1941 and 1945, cf. in particular, Fournier, "La banque en France", *Institutions et Mécanismes bancaires dans les pays de la CEE*, p. 70f; cf. also Raichlen, "La direction du crédit en France depuis la loi du 2 Decembre 1945", in *Droit Social*, February 1948; Dupont, *Le contrôle des banques et la direction du crédit en France*, pub. Dunod, Paris, 1952, p. 40f.; Spentsas, *Organisation et contrôle du crédit bancaire en France*, pub. Sirey, Paris, 1953, p. 30f.; Montfaion, *La nouvelle organisation du crédit en France et la nationalisation de certains établissements de crédit*, Paris, 1956; Wilson, "France", in *Banking in Western Europe*, Oxford University Press, London, 1962, p. 1-53; *Id.*, *French banking structure and credit policy*, Bell, London, 1957; Mitzakis, "Banking in France", *Comparative Banking*, Waterlow and Sons, London, 1963, p. 51f; Branger, *Traité d'économie bancaire*, vol. I, P.U.F., Paris, 1965, p. 77f.; Ruozi, *L'evoluzione strutturale e funzionale del sistema bancario francese*, Giuffré, Milan, 1966, p. 30, 59f.; Baudhuin, *Crédit et banque*, pub. Pichon, Paris, 1962; Petit-Dutaillis, *Le crédit et les banques*, pub. Sirey, Paris, 1963; Lammerskitten, *Das Französische Bankwesen*, Wiesbaden, 1967; Geis, *Struktur des Bankwesen in Frankreich*, Frankfurt am Main, 1971; D'Illiers and Norgenroth, "Das Bankwesen in Frankreich", in *Das Bankwesen im Grösseren Europa*, Baden-Baden, 1974, p. 259f.

3. On the nationalization of the banks in France, cf., apart from the

works quoted in the above notes, De Menthon, "La nationalisation du crédit", in *Droit Social*, September 1945; Grahame-Parker, "The Nationalisation of the French Banking System", in *The Banker*, January 1946; Cabrillac, "L'organisation du crédit et la nationalisation des banques", in *Semaine juridique*, 3 February 1946; Lhomme, "La nationalisation de la Banque de France et le contrôle du crédit", in *Annales de sciences économiques appliquées*, Louvain, April 1947; "La nationalisation des banques et du crédit en France", in *Les archives internationales*, November 1949; Hamel, "La nationalisation des grandes banques de dépots: quatre années d'experience", in *Droit Social*, January 1950.

4. Cf. Henrion: "A propos de la récente réforme bancaire en France", in *Revue de la banque*, no. 1 of 1966; Gerard, "Réforme de la réglementation bancaire (les décrets du 25 janvier 1966)", in *Banque*, March 1966.

5. Fournier, "La banque en France", *op. cit.*, p. 77f.

6. Cf. Duhamel, "L'institution en France du système des réserves obligatoires", in *Banque*, 1968, p. 177-182.

7. Fournier, "L'évolution des banques françaises", in *Banque*, September 1976, p. 830f.

8. Cf. Marion, "La fondation de la Banque de France et ses premières années", in *History of the Principal Public Banks*, p. 301-318; Potut, *La Banque de France*, Plon, Paris, 1961; Bolgert, "La Banque de France", in *Huit banques centrales européennes*, P.U.F., Paris, 1963; Millet, La Banque de France, IInd edition, Paris, 1964; *La Banque de France*, (joint work), pub. Berger-Levrault, Paris, 1975.

9. Cf. Patat, *Les banques centrales*, pub. Sirey, Paris, 1972, p. 31; La Banque de France (joint work), *op. cit.*, p. 221f.

10. Cf. Branger, *op. cit.*, p. 86; Fournier, "La banque en France", *op. cit.*, p. 128f.

11. For presentations of both of these viewpoints cf. respectively Branger, *op. cit.*, p. 89, and Fournier, *op. ult. cit.*, p. 131.

12. Cf. Branger, *op. cit.*, p. 90

13. Cf. Branger, *op. cit.*, p. 80f.

14. Cf. Fournier, *op. ult. cit.*, p. 74f.

15. Cf. Priouret, *La Caisse des dépôts*, P.U.F., Paris, 1966.

16. Cf Aymard, *La banque et l'Etat*, pub. Colin, Paris, 1960; Vasseur, *L'Etat banquier d'affaires*, pub. Dalloz, Paris, 1962; Chamas, *L'Etat et les systèmes bancaires contemporains*, pub. Sirey, Paris, 1965; Branger, *op. cit.*, p. 324f.

17. Branger, *op. cit.*, p. 82f.

18. Gavalda and Stoufflet, "Le secret bancaire en France", in *Le secret bancaire dans la CEE et en Suisse*, p. 78f.

V GREAT BRITAIN

1. GENERAL CHARACTERISTICS

Some authors fix the date of birth of the English banks around 1640, when following the seizure by King Charles I of their possessions in the form of precious metals which the merchants had deposited at the Tower of London, the latter took to the habit of entrusting their possessions to the goldsmiths: thus was born the custom of "Goldsmiths notes", which represent a considerable progress in the technique of paper currency.[1]

In any case, there is no doubt that the English banking system is the one that enjoys the highest prestige and the richest traditions.[2] It is characterized by a relative lack of laws, whose role is generally taken over by customs according to the principles of "common law". Even the principle of specialization of credit, characteristic of the English banking system, has its origin not in provisions of law, but in practical usage.

Another characteristic of the English banking system is that of flexibility in relations with the monetary authorities and the credit institutions. These relations are regulated according to the typically English principles, which have by now spread into all other countries, of "moral persuasion"[3] and "gentlemen's agreement".

In fact, making a comparison between the banking systems of continental Europe and that of England, the first thing to be noticed is that in the latter, notwithstanding its extremely efficient organization, the central Bank, in carrying out its supervisory duties over the banking system, limits itself to asking the banks for "information" and supplying them with "suggestions" and "recommendations".

Furthermore, it must be underlined that, in spite of the weakness of the British economy in the last twenty years, and in spite of the crisis which struck the secondary banks in 1974, the financial market of London is still the centre for the international capital market, above all because of the great freedom of operations which it can carry out: 244 foreign banks from 53 different countries are directly represented in the City while 91 foreign banks, though not directly represented, hold shares in London financial institutions set up by international banking groups.[4]

The City is also the most important centre for the gold market. Traditionally each morning at 10.30, the representatives of five firms, Rothschild, Samuel Montagu, Mocatta & Goldsmid, Johnson Matthey & Co., Sharps Pixley & Co., meet in a room of the London bank of Rothschild for the daily gold *fixing*. The fixing indicates the price at which the Bank of England, as mandatary of the federal reserve bank of South Africa, is prepared to sell gold. The Bank of England is present at the fixing through its authorized agent, i.e. the firm of Rothschild.

2. THE CENTRAL BANK

The banking, financial and commercial network of the country has its head in the City of London, the centre of a great tradition and high prestige, where all the most important financial institutions have their head-quarters.[5] Amongst these institutions, the Bank of England, set up in 1694, which may be considered as the first issuing bank in the true sense of the term, has a quite special importance.[6]

From its origin it was a private issuing bank whose capital was entirely subscribed by the public; only in 1928 did it acquire the monopoly of issue[7] and it is now the only issuer of currency notes.

Apart from its central office in the City, it possesses 8 branches in Birmingham, Bristol, Leeds, Liverpool, Manchester, Newcastle, Southampton and in London at the Law Courts.

In 1945, following the electoral success of the Labour Party, a bill for the nationalization of the Bank of England was presented by the Chancellor of the Exchequer, "in order to bring the Bank into public ownership and under public control".

The nationalization bill, approved by parliament, entered into force on 1 March 1946. On the same date, the old statute of the Bank, which went back to the XVIIth century, was replaced by a new statute.

The direction of the Bank is entrusted to the administrative Council which includes the governor, the vice-governor and 16 members, all nominated by the Crown.

As for control by the State, according to the "Bank of England Act" of 1946, the Treasury may give directions to the Bank;[8] however it appears that this power has not yet been used.

The Bank of England holds the accounts of the Public Treasury, of the discount enterprises, of the banks and of their residual private clientele; it is also charged with the administration of the public debt.

Following the nationalization act, its main role has become that of determining the country's monetary policy in agreement with the government. It also carries out ordinary banking operations, but in such a restricted measure that in practice this has lost all importance.

To facilitate economic and financial analyses, there is a conventional distinction between the Issue Department, which is considered as forming part of central government, and the Banking Department, which is considered as forming part of the banking sector.

3. THE LEGISLATIVE FRAME-WORK

In England there is no legal definition of bank.[9] Clearly there is a certain number of laws regarding banks and a certain number of institutions recognized as banks; however these laws refer to particular activities and the banks are only recognized as such within the limits set up by these laws.

Amongst the most important of these laws, the first that needs to be mentioned is the Exchange Control Act of 1947 which set up a list of banks (*authorized banks*) which were authorized to carry out exchange operations and to exercise certain powers delegated to them by the Act itself.

Furthermore, the Companies Act of 1948 requires the Board of Trade to set up a list of banks authorized to hold hidden reserves; such banks are known as the "Schedule 8 banks" and entry in this list has long been a sign of great prestige, whose importance was considerably diminished when the clearing banks decided to forego the privilege of hidden reserves. According to the same act, entry in the register of companies may be refused to enterprises which are considered as "undesirable". This provision has been used to limit the forming of new companies having the words "bank", "banker", etc. in their style; however such names cannot be prohibited for companies which were registered before 1948, nor to English branches of foreign companies.

Another Act that needs to be considered is the Protection of Depositors Act of 1963 which lays down particular conditions which must be respected by all companies which propose to advertise for the collection of deposits from the public. However, the banks may be exonerated by the Department of Trade from the observance of these conditions. The list of banks which were exonerated originally coincided with the list of schedule 8 banks, but, following the Companies Act of 1967, a new list of banks was set up called the "Section 127 banks": according to the latter law, only banks entered in this list may use the term "banks" and "banker" in their publicity for the collection of deposits.[10]

As we have seen, the Acts mentioned above provide for three different lists of banks, i.e. that of the *authorized banks*, that of the *schedule 8 banks* and that of the *section 127 banks*; apart from some exceptions, all the banks entered in one or more of these lists are included in the list of "statistical banks" held by the Bank of England. The statistical banks send statistical data periodically to the Bank of England so as to allow it to control the sector and furthermore they respect the ratio of 12% of obligatory reserves.

4. BANKS IN GREAT BRITAIN

The category of *statistical banks* includes:
(a)   the deposit banks, i.e. six *London clearing banks,* the three *Scottish clearing banks,*[11] the four *Northern Ireland banks,* and other deposit banks, five in number, forming a total of 18 deposit banks;
(b)   the *accepting houses,* 29 in number;
(c)   the *overseas banks,* the *consortium banks* and the *foreign banks* forming a total of about 200.

Amongst the clearing banks, the London "big four" (National Westminster Bank, Midland Bank, Barclays Bank and Lloyds Bank) occupy a special place, thanks to their enormous network of agencies and the very high number of deposits which they collect.

Also forming part of the banking sector, although they offer different services from the ordinary banks, are the 12 *discount houses,* which carry out the function of intermediaries on the monetary market between the Bank of England and the clearing banks. In fact the discount houses are true "wholesalers" in ready money and short term investments. Only these enterprises have access to the rediscount of the Bank of England, which, besides, reserves most of its operations on the open market for them.

Beside the banks proper and the discount houses, there is a certain number of so-called non-bank financial institutions (insurance companies, pension funds, building societies, unit trusts, investment trusts companies, etc.).

The Trustee Savings Banks, which appeared at the beginning of the XIXth century as philanthropic institutions, are not considered as forming part of the banking sector proper and are thus not required to hold reserves.[12] They are controlled by the Trustee Savings Bank Act of 1976 and are subject to the supervision of the monetary authorities. The savings banks, about 70 in number, collect savings deposits guaranteed by the State, which are lodged with the National Debt Commissioners to be invested in State bonds; thus they are considered as forming part of the public credit sector.

Also forming part of the public credit sector is the *National Savings Bank*, which has substituted the *Post Office Savings Bank* and offers services similar to those of the savings banks.

Still in the public sector is the *National Giro* which forms part of the postal administration and whose banking activities are controlled by the Treasury according to special laws.

The "special finance agencies", whose function is to grant particular credits difficult to obtain through traditional channels, also form part of the public sector. The most important are the *Agricultural Mortgage Corporation*, the *Commonwealth Development Finance Company*, the *Finance for Industry Limited* and the *Exporters Refinance Corporation*.

The Agricultural Mortgage Corporation, whose capital is shared between the Bank of England and 9 joint-stock banks, devotes itself to long term agricultural credit, while everyday agricultural credit is normally granted by the clearing banks and other credit institutions.

The Commonwealth Development Finance Company distributes credits for the development of the private sector in the countries of the Commonwealth.

The Finance for Industry Limited was set up in November 1973 following the merger between the *Finance Corporation for Industry* and the *Industrial and Commercial Finance Corporation* in order to finance industries of whatever size.

The Exporters Refinance Corporation was set up to supply a vast range of credits for exports. Still within the sector of financing exports, there is a public institution set up in 1919, the *Export Credit Guarantee Department*, which acts as an insurer in collaboration with the banks of the exporting enterprises.

5. CLEARING BANKS AND MERCHANT BANKS

As seen above, in England there is no legal definition of bank, so that any distinction between English banks is of necessity empirical. One of the most traditional distinctions is that between the clearing banks and the merchant banks, and it is based on their different historical origin.[13]

The *clearing banks* are deposit banks whose main activity consists of the collection of deposits and the granting of short term credits. Most of them are set up in the form of joint-stock banks and possess a vast network of agencies spread throughout the whole country. The clearing banks are those banks which take part in the *clearing* (or inter-bank clearing house) which is without doubt a typical institution of the English banking system. By "clearing" is meant the clearing of a large number of cheques amongst the members of a definite circle of participants, in the absence of which it would be necessary to transfer physically from one place to another a large amount of ready money. Originally, the first clearing house was founded in Edinburgh in 1760 while that of London was set up a few years later. In fact, at that time a prohibition was in force in London against the running of banks in the form of joint-stock companies;[14] as a result there was a large number of bankers who sent out their clerks every day to go round the other banks changing cheques and transforming them into ready money. These clerks, on their own initiative, took to the habit of meeting in a City tavern, the "Three Bells", to exchange cheques and to regulate the cash balance. In 1773 the bankers, who had become acquainted with this initiative, hired for their exclusive use a room of the tavern, which took the name of "clearing house". In 1833, because of the increased circulation of cheques, the room in the "Three Bells" became insufficient, a building called the "Clearing House" was built in Lombard Street, still inside the City.

The *merchant banks*, as their name indicates, are mostly family enterprises set up by merchant-bankers which go back to the end of the XVIIIth century and the XIXth century. The merchant banks properly so-called are *accepting houses*: in fact for several generations, their main activity consisted of the financing of commerce, which was mainly achieved by the "accepting" of bills of exchange.[15]

A certain number of merchant banks are members of the Issuing Houses Association: in fact the activity of the *Issuing Houses* goes back to the loans granted by them to foreign enterprises and governments. Later on the Issuing Houses also devoted themselves to the financing of English industry which previously had developed without recourse to the banking market.[16]

There are also merchant banks which are members both of the Accepting Houses Committee and the Issuing Houses Association.

At present, the differences between the clearing banks and the merchant banks have diminished; in fact, while previously the former did not carry out foreign financial operations, at present almost all have offices specializing in foreign business (foreign branches or overseas departments); as against this, a certain number of merchant banks have lost their original character of family enterprises to be transformed into joint-stock companies or to merge with other companies. In this respect it must be added that, if on the one hand the clearing banks devote themselves more and more often to medium and even long term credit, on the other hand the merchant banks also carry out short term operations.

In any case, the merchant banks are still a typical example of specialized banks whose sphere of activity consists above all in assistance and financial advising on the subject of mergers, acquisition of participations, etc.

Generally the merchant banks are similar to the French *banques d'affaires*; however in comparison with the latter, the English merchant banks collect few deposits and hold still fewer participations.

In Great Britain there is also a distinction between a "primary banking sector" composed of clearing banks, accepting houses, authorized banks and banks which are voluntarily subject to the control of the Bank of England, and a "secondary banking sector" (*fringe banks*) formed of a large number of bank-type enterprises which devote themselves above all to the collection of short term deposits on the monetary market to use them in real estate investment operations, in medium and long term mortgage loans and for private credits. These enterprises had a spectacular development at the beginning of the seventies, thanks in part to building speculation which allowed them to realize extremely high profits; on the other hand, since 1973, above all because of the crisis in the building sector, they have mostly found themselves in serious financial difficulties, so that the large deposit banks, in agreement with the Bank of England, have been forced to intervene so as to ensure a recovery in the administration of the enterprises in difficulty.[17]

6. THE PROFESSIONAL ASSOCIATIONS

Although membership of the professional associations is optional, almost all the statistical banks are members of the *British Bankers Association* which in its turn belongs to the Banking Federation of the EEC.

However there are other representative associations which include a more restricted number of members: such are the *Committee of Scottish Clearing Banks*, the *Accepting Houses Committee* (which includes most of the accepting houses) and the *London Discount Market Association* (which includes most of the London discount houses). In London there is also the *Committee of London Clearing Bankers* closely associated with the British Bankers Association. None of these banking associations has a formal role in the system of supervision of the banking sector; however they may be consulted when measures of monetary policy are adopted which concern the banking sector.

7. MERGERS AND ACQUISITION OF PARTICIPATIONS

There is no limit to the acquisition by banks of participations in enterprises other than credit institutions; however, the banks hold relatively few participations in other companies. As against this, the Bank of England exercises a control over all banking mergers which is anything but formal. For this purpose, a merger is considered as being the acquisition of participations in another bank above the limit of 15% of its captital.[18]

Banking mergers, in common with mergers between other companies, are subject to the provisions of the Fair Trading Act of 1973 according to which, when the property of a company which intends to merge is above 5,000,000 pounds, the Secretary of State for prices and consumer protection may submit the case to the Monopolies and Mergers Commission, which is competent to decide if the proposed merger conforms with public interest. In any case, a planned merger regarding banks is preliminarily examined by the Treasury and the Bank of England which may express its disapproval when it considers that the decision of the Monopolies and Mergers Commission could be unfavourable.

However, if the operation conforms with the legal provisions on the subject of mergers, the Bank of England does not oppose the acquisition of participations (whatever their amount) by an English bank or by a bank from another country of the EEC in another English bank, even if the latter is an accepting house, provided however that there is an amicable agreement between the banks participating in the operation.

As against this, the Bank of England is on principle against the acquisition of participations in a statistical bank above the limit of 15% by a bank from a country not belonging to the European Economic Community.

Lastly it must be mentioned that, in order to benefit from certain exemptions, the banks must amongst other things inform the Department of Trade of any transfer of shares above 25% of capital.

8. BRANCH OFFICES

There is no limitation to the opening of agencies by banks registered in Great Britain.

It must however be specified that, according to the Exchange Control Act of 1947, any company which intends to carry out exchange operations or open current accounts for non-residents, must obtain authorization from the Treasury. Thus, banks which are not registered in Great Britain cannot obtain such authorization if they do not already have a branch office in London.

There is no limitation to the opening of branches abroad by English banks although the Bank of England always wishes to be informed; furthermore, the latter is not pleased if an English bank, by means of a branch office abroad carries out particular activities for which it is not authorized in Great Britain.

9. NECESSARY REQUIREMENTS FOR THE EXERCISE OF BANKING ACTIVITIES

In Great Britain, apart from some exceptions like for example the Building Societies, institutions which collect deposits do not need to seek any authorization before beginning activities; furthermore there are no particular provisions governing their administration.

However, for many years now the Bank of England has applied a system of bank supervision and this role, although it has no origin in law, has been unanimously accepted by the banks forming part of the so-called primary banking sector. Thus, in practice, institutions intending to obtain the statute of statistical banks conform to the directives of the Bank of England, according to which they must take the form of limited companies. There is only one ancient statistical bank which preserves its original form of company with unlimited liability.

Although there are no means to prevent the access of an individual to the banking sector, the latter may not however receive any official recognition.

In Great Britain there are no banks set up in the form of cooperative societies. However, there is a small number of credit and health insurance institutions (e.g. the *friendly societies*) which are not, though, recognized officially.

For the purposes of recognition according to section 123 of the Companies Act of 1967, the Department of Trade imposes on the banks a minimum disposition of fully paid up capital of 150,000 pounds. To form part of the statistical banks, the Bank of England requires that the institutions concerned dispose of a minimum fully paid up capital of one million pounds. It must be specified that these figures are determined administratively and may thus be modified according to the requirements of monetary policy or in particular situations.

There is no limitation to the number of administrators and managers of banking institutions, nor is there any limitation of this type for enterprises belonging to other economic sectors.

In the month of August 1976, the government presented to Parliament a draft bill for banking reform according to which institutions intending to collect deposits must obtain prior authorization from the Bank of England; and to this end they must dispose of a minimum capital and reserves. Protection of the name "bank", etc. is also provided for.

This new system of supervision of the banking sector will not apply to savings banks, building societies, the National Savings Bank or the National Giro, nor to the friendly societies which are already subject to a special control. Since the savings banks tend more and more to offer the same services as the banks, the government intends, in the near future, to subject them to the same provisions as govern the banks.

10. THE SYSTEM OF SUPERVISION

According to section four of the Bank of England Act of 1946, the Bank of England, "if they think it necessary in the public interest, may request information from and make recommendations to bankers, and may, if so authorized by the Treasury, issue directions to any banker for the purpose of securing that effect is given to any such request or recommendation"; however these powers have never been exercised, since the central Bank has always preferred, in the fulfilment of monetary policy and in the exercise of its powers of control over the banks and other fiancial institutions, to have recourse to voluntary and spontaneous collaboration.[19]

Still in the same section, it is laid down that the Bank of England may demand the examination of the books of any bank so as to proceed to an audit; however this power has never been exercised and it is considered as a measure to be applied in exceptional cases. In any case, there is no official recognition of the Bank of England's power to inspect banks.

On the other hand, the Companies Act of 1948 lays down that the Department of Trade has the power to nominate inspectors charged with the supervision of the business of companies, while the Consumer Credit Act of 1974 lays down that the Director General of Fair Trading has the power to investigate operations carried out in violation of the latter law.

As for the Bank of England's control over banking activities, it must be remembered that here the control system is traditionally flexible, personalized and participative, in the sense that, due to the lack of legislative sanctions, the supervision of the Bank of England must be voluntarily accepted by the banks concerned.

Thus a system of extremely flexible ratios was already in force in 1975 when it was substituted by a relatively more rigid system.

In any case, the Bank of England has always been clearly opposed to a system of rigid ratios to be imposed compulsorily and at the same time for all banks, preferring rather, according to the circumstances, to give advice to each bank on the relation between capital and reserves on the one hand and their employment on the other.

11. THE REFORM BILL

Recently, following difficulties that had arisen in the sector of British secondary banks, and which had shown up the weak points of British banking legislation and, particularly, of the system of supervision and control, the government published a "white paper" on credit reform in Great Britain. It is a draft bill for banking reform which contains important innovations for the whole banking system.

The essential points of this reform consist of the setting up of an obligatory fund for the guarantee of deposits; of the introduction of a generalized regime of prior authorizations for all institutions which collect deposits; of the protection of the name "bank" etc.; of the reinforcement and widening of the Bank of England's control powers; of the fixing by the Bank of England, in agreement with the Treasury, of certain ratios; etc.

As for the guarantee fund, the study Commission for the reform proposed that this protection be assured for all deposits up to 10,000 pounds entrusted to authorized institutions.

As for the conditions for admission to banking activities, it was proposed to establish for all banks set up in the form of commercial companies a minimum capital and a system of obligatory reserves, as well as requiring guarantees of qualification and professional respectability from their directors which will be checked by the Bank of England. In case of refusal or withdrawal of license by the Bank of England, the possibility of presenting an appeal to the Treasure is provided for.

When this reform enters into force, it will entail an alignment of British banking legislation with that of most of the countries of the EEC.

12. THE STOCK-EXCHANGE IN GREAT BRITAIN

The control of the English stock-exchange is without doubt the most typical example of self-discipline within a sectoral organization. The English stock-exchanges are set up as private associations; in particular they are institutions set up in the form of joint-stock companies to which are also entrusted functions of public concern.[20]

No provisions have been issued by the public authorities on the organization and functioning of the stock-exchange; nor is any official control by the State over the stock-exchange provided for: the only intervention by the public authorities arises through the Government Broker who is a member by right of the Council of the Stock-Exchange. All the rules and regulations governing the market of stocks and shares derive from the Council of the Stock-Exchange.

Only individuals possessing at least one and at most 200 shares in the stock-exchange may be members; thus the possession of these shares attributes at the same time the status of share-holder and that of member of the stock-exchange.

There is a distinction between those who carry out the activities of intermediary on the London Stock-Exchange, i.e. the brokers and the jobbers: the jobbers are intermediaries who never have direct contact with the public, but exclusively with the brokers; they specialize in certain categories of securities (for example the beer, chemical, electrical, mechanical industries, etc.) which they acquire and sell to the brokers when the latter ask for them on behalf of the public.

It must be remembered that the London Stock-Exchange is the second most important in the world after that of New York.[21] In 1967 there were about 3300 stock-brokers in the London Stock-Exchange, but their number has steadily diminished since they tend to regroup in larger societies.

As for the admission of stock and shares to quotation, it is the competence of the Committee on quotation which is an organization of a private type created directly by the stock-exchange operators.

Unlike in other countries (for example Holland and Germany) the commercial banks do not have any direct relation with the stock-exchange, nor do they have their own representatives participating in meetings.

13. THE PROTECTION OF BANKING SECRECY

In England, there is no control over, nor legal definition of banking secrecy. However its recognition and protection are not placed in doubt and derive from a decision of 1924 (Taurnier v. National Provincial Bank, 1924, I.K.B. 461).

As a matter of principle, the banks are required to supply to the judicial and administrative authorities any information about the accounts of their clients whenever there is an order from the Tribunal to this effect, whenever the banks are called to witness or whenever the banks consider that the information requested is "in the public interest". Thus for example, in the case of divorce, the Court may ask the bank for an extract of the husband's various accounts, as well as a list of the stocks in portfolio which he has deposited, so as to establish the amount of alimony should there be suspicion that the husband has not declared his true income.

As for banking secrecy in relation to the revenue authorities, the latter address themselves initially to the banks and, on the basis of "public interest", ask for information on their clients' accounts. Since the banks do not generally comply with these requests, the revenue authorities may impose a very high tax on the reluctant tax payer. In this case the tax payer may make an appeal to a body called the Special Commissioners, but the latter may then order the bank to produce the tax payer's accounts for inspection.

NOTES

1. Cf. Orsingher, *Les banques dans le monde*, Paris, 1964, p. 41.
2. On the English banking system in general, cf. Mannig Dacey, *The British banking mechanism*, 5th ed., London, 1964; Mackenzie, *Banking systems of Great Britain, France, Germany and the U.S.A.*, London, 1960; Wadsworth, "Banking system of the United Kingdom of Great Britain and Northern Ireland", in *Banking systems*, Columbia University Press, New York, 1959, p. 769-839; Auburn, "Banking in the U.S.A. and the U.K.", *Comparative Banking*, 2nd ed., London, 1963; Pringle, *A guide to banking in Britain*, pub. Charles Knight, London, 1973; Revell, *The British Financial System*, pub. Macmillan, London, 1973; European Communities, *Monetary policy in the countries of the EEC*, 1974 supplement, Brussels, 1974; Britisch Bankers Association, *Prudential regulation of Credit Institutions in the E.E.C.: United Kingdom*, London, 1975; Morgan, Harrington & Zis, *Banking Systems and Monetary Policy in the E.E.C.*, pub. The Financial Times Ltd., London 1974; Campbell, "Das Bankwesen in Grossbritannien" in *Das Bankwesen im grösseren Europa*, Baden-Baden, 1974, p. 297f.; Forrest, *An Analysis of Banking Structures in the European Community*, published by the Banker Research Unit,

London, 1974; Hein, *Struktur des Bankwesen in Grossbritannien*, Frankfurt am Main, 1968.

3. On "moral persuasion" as a technique for the control of banks, cf. in general Aschheim, *Techniques of Monetary Control*, pub. The Johns Hopkins Press, Baltimore, 1961, p. 99-100.

4. Cf. Dhom, "Rôle des centres financiers en Europe", in *L'orientation des mouvements internationaux des capitaux*, Luxemburg, 1974, p. 32f.; Fair, "Clearing Banks and the Common Market", in *The three banks review*, 1973, p. 55.

5. Clarke, *The City in the world economy*, London, 1965.

6. On the Bank of England, cf. Clapham, *The Bank of England*, Cambridge, 1944; Richards, "The first fifty years of the Bank of England", *History of the principal public banks*, p. 201f,; Institute of Bankers, *The Bank of England today*, London, 1964.

7. Before that time there had been a few private banks also issuing notes.

8. Cf. Section 4 of the 1946 Bank of England Act: "The Treasury may from time to time give such directions to the Bank as, after consultation with the Governor of the Bank, they think necessary in the public interest".

9. However, to be a banker a significant proportion of his business must be:
(i) conduct of current accounts (including deposit accounts);
(ii) collection of cheques;
(iii) payment of cheques.
Cf. United Dominions Trust v. Kirkwood, 1965.

10. Other acts may be mentioned dealing with particular banking activities, as follows:
(a) The Moneylenders Act of 1900 to 1927;
(b) The Prevention of Fraud (Investments) Act, 1958;
(c) The Building Societies Act, 1962;
(d) The Income and Corporation Taxes Act, 1970;
(e) The Consumer Credit Act, 1974.

11. On the Scottish banks, cf. Gaskin, *The Scottish Banks*, London, 1965,

12. On the Savings Banks, cf. Horne, *History of Savings Banks*, Oxford, 1947; Lawton, *Guide to the law of Trustee Savings Banks*, 3rd. ed., London, 1962.

13. Cf. Stechov, *Die Auflösung der Arbeitsteilung im englischen Bankensystem*, Würzburg, 1973.

14. The first English banks set up in the form of joint-stock banks arose half way through the XIXth century.

15. Cf. Macartney-Filgate, "Merchant and other banking houses", in *The City of London as a centre of International Trade and Finance*, London, 1961; Reid, *The role of the Merchant Banks today*, pub. The Institute of Bankers, London, 1963; Wechsberg, *The Merchant Bankers*, Weidenfeld & Nicholson, London.

16. Cf. Tyser, *The work of an Issuing House*, pub. The Institute of Bankers, London, 1951.

17. Deguen & David, "Les mesures prises pour renforcer les garanties de liquidité et de solvabilité des institutions financières", *Banque*, 1976, p. 940f.

18. Cf. Bank of England, "Banking Mergers and Participations", in *Quarterly Bulletin*, December 1972.

19. Cf. Bank of England, *Quarterly Bulletin*, June 1975.

20. On the London Stoch-Exchange, cf. Wincott, *The Stock-Exchange*, London, 1948; Ritchie, "The London Stock-Exchange and International Investment", in *The City of London as a centre of International Trade and Finance*, London, 1961; Morgan & Thomas, *The Stock-Exchange— its history and functions*, London, 1962.

21. The New York Stock-Exchange, i.e. the mythical Wall Street Stock-Exchange, was born in 1792 when 24 merchants of the area met under a plane tree which happened to be just there, and signed an agreement according to which they undertook to set up a centralized market for the buying and selling of securities.

VI GERMANY

1. GENERAL CHARACTERISTICS

In Germany, the modern banks arose half way through the XIXth century, together with the industrialization of the country and the resulting requirements of capital;[1] however, in order to examine the present organization of the German banking system, it is necessary to consider in particular the situation of the country immediately after the second world war, when the banking structures of the country were deeply modified.[2]

In 1946, after 70 years of existence, the *Reichsbank* was suppressed, and its disappearance was followed by the progressive creation of regional issuing banks *(Landeszentralbanken)* in each of the 11 *Länder* of the new German Federal Republic, coordinated by the *Bank Deutscher Länder*, in accordance with the wishes of the victorious allies who favoured deconcentration.[3]

In 1957, following the merger of the 11 regional central banks with the Bank Deutscher Länder, the *Deutsche Bundesbank* was founded and its central office was placed in Frankfurt am Main. However, the 11 Landeszentralbanken still survive, with the same name, as administrative offices of the central bank.[4]

As for German banking legislation, the following need special mention:

(1) The Act of 21 June 1948;
(2) The Act of 26 July 1957;
(3) The Act of 10 July 1961 relating to the organization of the banking profession *(Gesetz über das Kreditwesen)*;
(4) The Act concerning joint-stock companies of 6 September 1965;

(5) The Act of 1967 on stability and economic expansion, which, amongst other things, gave to the federal government the power to limit, with a decree approved by the *Bundesrat*, the recourse to credit by the federal State, the *Länder*, the municipalities and associations of municipalities, as well as by special public funds and associations in public law pursuing some particular object;

(6) The Act of 24 March 1976 containing amendments to the law concerning the organization of the banking profession.

2. MONETARY POLICY AND CENTRAL BODIES; THE CENTRAL BANK

In Germany, responsibility concerning monetary policy is, in principle, the competence of the central government, but in fact it is shared between the government and the *Deutsche Bundesbank*. The latter has greater responsibility concerning credit policy, while the control of the banking profession is the competence of the Federal Office for Control of the Banks *(Bundesaufsichtsamt für Kreditwesen)* which acts in close collaboration with the *Bundesbank*.

The German Federal Bank *(Deutsche Bundesbank)*, set up by the Act of 26 July 1957, is the central institution of banking organization in West Germany.[5] It has progressively taken over the functions of the Reichsbank, it has the privilege of issuing bank notes and has the duty of watching over the stability of the currency both at home and abroad, conserving its power to acquire the currency and regulating the circulation of paper money and the granting of credits.

As for the principal means at the disposal of the Bank for the fulfilment of its duties, it is necessary to mention the fixing of the discount rate, the imposition of obligatory reserves on credit institutions and open market operations.

Since its origin, the Bank has been an institution under public law of which the State holds all the capital; however, it carries out its assignments in full independence from the orientations of the federal government since it only has the obligation of upholding the general economic policy of the government, so that it may be considered as being the most independent of the European central banks.[6]

The Bundesbank holds the accounts of the federal Treasury and of the Treasuries of the *Länder*, as well as those of the public administrations and local collectives. Another of its assignments is the service of inter-bank clearing.

The Central Council *(Zentralbankrat)* is the body which determines the general policy of the Bank, while the directorate *(Direktorium)* is charged with its execution. The General Council is presided over by the President of the *Bundesbank* and is composed of the members of the directorate and the presidents of the Länderszentralbanken. All members of the Council are nominated by the president of the Federal Republic, the members of the directorate on the proposal of the federal government and the presidents of the Landeszentralbanken on the proposal of the Bundesrat which is the parliamentary representation of the Länder.

Members of the federal government have the right to participate in meetings of the Central Council of the Bank, but they do not dispose of the right to vote. As against this, the president of the Bundesbank must be invited to participate in all meetings of the Council of Ministers in which questions relating to monetary policy are discussed.

3. STRUCTURE OF THE BANKING SYSTEM

In general, the type of bank prevailing in Germany is that of the so-called universal or mixed bank which may devote itself to any type of banking operation.[7]

The banks operating in Germany may be divided into three categories:

(a) The banks in the private sector (credit banks and mortgage banks);

(b) The banks in the public sector (savings banks, bank-giro offices, etc.);
(c) The banks set up in the form of cooperative associations
(popular banks and *Raiffeisen* banks).

(a) *The banks in the private sector*

The banks belonging to the private sector may in their turn be classified into three groups:
(1) the three large banks (*Deutsche Bank, Dresdner Bank* and
Commerzbank) whose activity at the operative level extends over
the whole federal territory; they are all set up in the form of joint-
stock companies and dispose of about 3,000 agencies and a large
number of branches abroad;
(2) the regional and local banks, about one hundred in number,
with a total of about 2,600 agencies, which may take on the legal
form of joint-stock companies, of limited partnerships or of limited
liability companies;
(3) the other credit institutions, including mortgage banks, which
specialize in the concession of first mortgages, and individual enterprises (*Privatbankiers*).

The number of private banks, which have a long tradition in Germany, has continually diminished: in 1928 there were more than
2,000, in 1939 less than 1,000 and half way through the sixties
about 250, but following an ever more marked process of concentration, their number has been further reduced to the point that in
1975 only 130 private banks were still active.

(b) *The banks in the public sector*

Amongst the credit institutions belonging to the public sector, the
first that should be mentioned are the real estate credit institutions
under public law, which are subject to the Act of 21 December

1927 on mortgage bonds and the bonds of public credit institutions, which was modified in 1963.

The credit institutions belonging to the sector of savings banks should also be mentioned, i.e. the savings banks properly so-called and the bank-giro offices functioning as centres for the settlement of the accounts of their affiliates, which in the course of the last 50 years have acquired a great importance.

The savings banks (*Sparkassen*) which were previously limited in general to receiving savings deposits and granting long term loans, devote themselves more and more to short term operations, both in the collection of deposits and the concession of credits. Furthermore, the savings banks play an important role in financing the construction of habitations. Although they devote themselves in the first place to satisfying the financial needs of the middle classes, the most important of them, and above all their central bodies, i.e. the bank-giro offices (*Girozentralen*), devote themselves to a considerable extent to the concession of large credits, the financing of industry and the formation of issuing syndicates.

The *Girozentralen* (clearing houses) represent a special type of credit institution. Historically, their origin is based on the idea of the savings banks that due to competition it is necessary to have one's own clearing system for bank transfers. For this purpose, besides the already existing savings banks' associations, clearing banks' associations under public law were founded. These clearing banks' associations established the *Girozentralen* whose functions should be to serve as central clearing agencies for noncash transactions between the savings banks. Further, they should be responsible for the evening-up between the savings banks, for assuring the liquidity of the savings banks in pressure periods, and for further services to the savings banks organization, performing the functions of a central savings bank.[8]

At present, there are 750 savings banks which dispose of about 16,000 agencies and 12 *Girozentralen* at whose head is the *Deutsche Girozentrale*.

(c) *The banks set up in the form of cooperative associations*

Although they perform an exclusively local activity, the cooperative credit banks (*Kreditgenossenschaften*) play an important role in the German banking system.

There is a distinction between the commercial credit cooperatives and the agricultural credit cooperatives. The first are also called popular banks (*Volksbanken*), they are about 700 in number and dispose of about 2,500 agencies; the second, called Raiffeisen banks (*Raiffeisenkassen*) from the name of the founder of the system, Friedrich Wilhelm-Raiffeisen, are about 9,000.

The cooperative credit banks are organized according to the Act of 1 May 1889 on cooperatives, modified by an act of 1898; they must conform to the provisions of the law concerning the banking profession.

At the head of the cooperative banking organization is the *Deutsche Genossenschaftskasse*, a body under public law founded in 1949 in Frankfurt am Main. This body has the right to issue bonds and may grant long term credits to affiliated banks.

4. MERGERS AND ACQUISITION OF PARTICIPATIONS

In the German banking law (KWG) there is no provision concerning the participation of banks in enterprises other than the banks themselves, if one excepts art. 12 according to which "the total amount of a credit institution's durable investments in the form of land, real estate, ships and *participations* calculated according to their book value, may not exceed the total of their own funds. The federal control office may, on demand, authorize a credit institution to depart provisionally from this provision".

The concept of participation remains undefined. For the compilation of the annual balances of credit institutions, the principle of art. 152 of the law on joint-stock companies is adopted according to which participations are considered as being shares in the capital of companies above the level of 25%.

At present, the reform Act of 1976 forces the banks to declare the permanent acquisition and the transfer of a participation to another credit institution, as well as variations in the amount of the participation when this exceeds 5% of capital. The holding of registered shares above the level of 10% of the capital of an enterprise is considered as a participation (art. 24, section I, no. 3).

As for banking mergers, although there is no need for any authorization, any credit institution intending to merge with another credit institution must advise the federal control office and the Deutsche Bundesbank in good time.

5. ACCESS TO BANKING ACTIVITIES; THE OPENING OF AGENCIES AND BRANCHES

Anyone proposing to carry out banking operations as defined by art. 1, section I of the law on the organization of the banking profession must obtain written authorization from the Federal Control Office. The latter, in granting authorization, may impose particular obligations within the frame-work of the objectives pursued by the aforesaid law, and also limit the authorization to particular banking operations (art. 32 KWG).

According to the Reform Act of 1976, before granting authorization, the Federal Control Office is now required to consult the banking association concerned (art. 32 subsection III). The decision of the Federal Control Office on the granting of authorization may however differ from the opinion expressed by the banking association concerned.

Authorization may only be refused in the case in which the funds destined for the exercise of banking activities, and in particular own resources, are considered insufficient, or else in the case in which the promotors and director do not possess the professional qualifications and respectability necessary for the running of a credit institution (art. 33 KWG).

As for the minimum capital required, it has been increased recently from 3 million marks to 6 million marks.

Unlike in other countries, for example Italy and France, the authority competent to grant the aforesaid authorization may not reject the application on the grounds that it does not appear justified by general or local economic necessities. Equally, this reason may not justify the denial of authorization for a branch of a bank belonging to a country of the EEC or the USA.

In Germany there are no limitations as to the legal form of banks, but, according to the Reform Act of 1976, an individual enterprise is no longer permitted to run banking business, since in the case of a single entrepreneur, it is not possible to make a clear distinction between private property and the property of the enterprise; and furthermore the capital destined for the running of the banking enterprise is exposed to the claims of the bankers' private creditors. On the other hand, the principle of "four eyes", introduced by the same reform act, according to which a credit institution must be run by at least two persons who must take on the running not only as a courtesy title, could not operate in relation to an individual enterprise. However this provision does not apply to persons who, at the time when the reform law came into force were already carrying out banking activities in the form of individual enterprises.

Authorization for the exercise of banking activities is withdrawn when use is not made of it for a period of one year from its concession.

Furthermore the Federal Control Office may withdrawn authorization:

(1)   when it has been obtained on the basis of erroneous or incomplete information or by fraud, threat, or other unfair means;

(2)   when the activity constituting the object of the authorization has not been exercised for a period of one year;

(3)   when the Federal Control Office becomes acquainted with facts from which it may be deduced the the conditions of respectability and professional qualification required for the running of a credit institution are not respected;

(4)   when the safety of deposits entrusted to the credit institution is endangered and this danger cannot be avoided by other measures.

In this respect, it should be taken into consideration that the reform law of 1976 not only provided for extra motives which can entail the withdrawal of authorization for violation of the principle of "four eyes" and for violation of the ban on exercising banking activities in the form of an individual enterprise, but also specified conditions which can entail both the withdrawal of authorization for risks deriving from a credit institution's inability to satisfy its creditors, and the closure of the same institute. By analogy with art. 92, subsection I of the law on joint-stock companies it is considered that the safety of deposits entrusted to credit institutions is endangered when the institution has undergone an important loss or is functioning permanently without any assets. For this purpose, the legislator uses the criterion of loss of half of own funds, or, respectively, of losses of more than 10% of own funds during three consecutive financial years (art. 35, sub-section II, no. 5).

The credit institutions are required to declare immediately to the Federal Control Office and to the Deutsche Bundesbank the opening, transfer or closure of an agency; but they are not required to seek any authorization for the opening of agencies and branches. Furthermore there is no restriction on German banks regarding the opening of branches abroad.

As for the control of foreign banks, they are subject to the same regime as the German banks, except for the fact that authorization for the exercise of banking activities may be refused when it is not justified by general economic necessities. However the latter limitation does not apply to banks originating from EEC countries or the USA.

The names "bank", "banker" and "savings bank" are protected by the law relating to the organization of the banking profession.

6. THE SUPERVISION AND CONTROL OF THE BANKING SECTOR; THE NEW PROVISIONS OF THE ACT OF 1976

In Germany, the control and supervision of the banking sector are ensured by the Federal Control Office (*Bundesaufsichtsamt für*

Kreditwesen), whose central office is in Berlin and of which the Deutsche Bundesbank is the active agent.

The control system was considerably modified by the Act of 24 March 1976 containing amendments to the law on the organization of the banking profession.

These amendments, suggested by the events that accompanied the bankruptcy of the Herstatt bank and by other difficulties which have arisen recently, regard in particular the limitation of risks deriving from credit operations, the reinforcement of the powers of the control authority and some extra regulations added to the system of deposit insurance characteristic of the banking profession.

The legislator, bearing in mind the fact that most bankruptcies of banks which have occurred since 1962 were related to large credits that could not be recovered, and in order to limit the risks of credit institutions, has laid down the following limits:

(1) no large credit (including the opening of credit lines) may exceed 75% of the amount of own funds of the credit institution (art. 13, sub-section IV);

(2) the five largest credits (including the opening of credit lines) may not exceed three times the own capital of the credit institution concerned (art. 13, sub-section III);

(3) the total amount of large credits (only credits actually contracted) may not exceed eight times the own capital of the credit institution concerned (art. 13, sub-section III);

(4) in calculating large credits, the guarantees furnished for the concession of credit according to art. 19, sub-section I, nos. 1-3 are upheld for the full amount (art. 13, sub-section VI) while previously they were upheld only for 50%.

Furthermore, according to art. 33, sub-section I, no. 4, it is required that a credit institution be run by at least two persons who must take on its running not only as a courtesy title (principle of "four eyes").

In fact, given that the activities of single entrepreneurs outside of banking affairs and the risks which thus arise cannot be adequately controlled by the supervision authorities, single entrepreneurs are no longer permitted to run banking enterprises.

As for the powers of control properly so called, the legislator, in order to ensure that the Federal Control Office and the Bundesbank become fully acquainted with events regarding the credit institutions and their administrators, has modified a whole series of obligations to notify or to declare, or has introduced them *ex novo*. Thus for example, all credit institutions are required, according to art. 26, sub-section I, and by analogy with the provisions of art. 148 of the Act on joint-stock companies, to work out the annual balance sheet and the account of profits and losses within the first three months following the end of the financial year in order to remit them to the Deutsche Bundesbank.

Art. 44, sub-section I now allows the Federal Control Office to proceed to audits of credit institutions even without a specific motive, while previously the right to carry out audit of credit institutions was only recognized in particular cases. Since these audits will be carried out for all credit institutions and with a certain regularity, they will be almost institutionalized and the Federal Control Office will thus have at its disposal an extremely efficient instrument for the supervision of banks.

As for measures to be applied in case of urgency, the Federal Control Office may order provisionally a moratorium on all credit institutions with negative balance sheet (art. 46, letter a). As a complement to this, art. 46, letter b lays down that only the Federal Control Office is qualified to request the opening of bankruptcy proceedings.

7. THE SYSTEM OF OBLIGATORY RESERVES

In the German Federal Republic, the vast majority of credit institutions is subject to the obligation to hold reserves. According to art. 16, sub-section I of the Act of 26 July 1957 on the Deutsche Bundesbank, as modified on 22 July 1969, so as to act on the circulation of paper money and the distribution of credit, the Deutsche Bundesbank has the right to demand that the credit institutions keep certain sums tied up as minimum reserves to the level of a certain percentage of their current liabilities resulting both from demand depositits, period deposits and savings deposits, and from short and medium term loans, with the exception of engagements with respect to other credit institutions who are also obliged to maintain minimum reserves. The percentage of reserves may not exceed 30% of demand obligations, 20% of period obligations and 10% of savings deposits. However within these limits, the Bundesbank may vary the percentages according to certain general criteria, and above all according to the different categories of credit institutions.

To apply the provision relating to obligatory reserves, the Bundesbank publishes "directives concerning obligatory reserves" which supply all the details on the obligation to hold reserves, and on the amount of the sums to be deposited for this purpose. Each annual report includes the text of the directives to be applied on the subject of minimum reserves and any modification is immediately published in the Official Journal of the Federal State.

By virtue of the provisions issued by the Bundesbank, the sums constituting obligatory reserves do not produce interest. The credit institutions subject to the regime of reserves thus suffer a loss of income which is greater or smaller according to the size of the reserve ratios which have been applied to them. For this reason, the policy followed by the Bundesbank on the subject of obligatory reserves not only has a quantitative effect on banking liquidity, but also influences interest rates. Thus for example, in the case of an increase in minimum reserves, the banks seek to compensate for the corresponding loss of income above all by raising the cost of money for their clientele.[9]

8. THE SYSTEM OF DEPOSIT INSURANCE

After the crisis of the Herstatt bank, the federal government at first intended to introduce a joint and several mechanism for deposit guarantee to include all credit institutions.

Following the opposition of the professional associations of the banks, the government abandoned the original project for the legal control of deposit guarantee and recognized that a free guarantee mechanism, on the initiative of the various associations, would conform better to the legal and economic regime established in Germany. For this reason, the reform law of 1976 only contains some dispositions of a marginal character on this point, whose purpose is to back up the institutional guarantee measures adopted by the representative associations of the credit institutions.

The central nucleus of the new mechanism is formed by the "deposit guarantee fund" of the Federal Association of German Banks which earlier on ran the "urgency fund".[10]

While the old urgency fund only guaranteed deposits up to a level of 20,000 marks, the new fund now guarantees the whole amount of deposits lodged by non-banking clientele, with the exclusion of deposits lodged by persons holding more than 50% of the capital of a credit institution and the deposits of administrators. The guarantee "platform", for each depositant, corresponds to 30% of own funds of the bank in difficulty.

9. THE STOCK-EXCHANGE IN GERMANY

In the Federal Republic and in West Berlin there are eight stock-exchanges (Berlin, Bremen, Dusseldorf, Frankfurt, Hamburg, Hanover, Munich, Stuttgart): amongst these the markets of Dusseldorf and Frankfurt am Main are the most important, while the Frankfurt stock-exchange is also the most ancient German stock-exchange.

The German stock-exchanges are institutions under public law. The basic law on the stock-exchanges goes back to 1896 and has been modified several times, in particular in 1908, in 1963 and in 1968.

Each stock-exchange has its own internal regulations which are approved by the government of the *Land* where it has its seat.

The organization and functioning of the stock-exchange are the competence of the board of directors of the stock-exchange (*Bör-senvorstand*).

The supervision of the running of the stock-exchange is entrusted to a government commissioner nominated by the government of the *Land*.

The credit institutions play a predominant role on the market of stocks and shares, since only the representatives of the banks are allowed to operate on the stock-exchange. They operate both on behalf of their clientele and on their own account, since there is no ban on the acquisition of shares and participations in industrial enterprises.

In Germany, the stock-exchanges (i.e. the market of fixed income stocks and variable income securities) are not subject to any restrictive disposition limiting their access in a general manner or for certain categories of issues. Generally speaking, it is issuing syndicates that issue stocks and bonds.

10. THE PROTECTION OF BANKING SECRECY

In German law, there is no control over, nor legal definition of banking secrecy.[11] Nevertheless, the preface to the general conditions (*Allgemeine Geschätsbedingungen*) recalls the fact that business relations between banks and clients are founded on trust, thus posing the fundamental principle of the banks' obligation to maintain professional secrecy.[12]

Although the banks are required by law to communicate certain information to the supervisory authorities, according to art. 9 of the Banking Act of 1961, the members of the Federal Control Office, as well as the staff in the service of the Deutsche Bundesbank are required to respect professional secrecy.

According to the most authorative doctrine,[13] violation of the obligation to maintain secrecy is justified only:

(a)   by public interest in the good state of the economy;

(b)   in the interests of the banking profession;

(c)   in the interests of economic operators, with particular refer-

ence to information supplied by the banks;
(d)   in revenue matters, in the interests of the good running of the economy, but not in all cases.

NOTES

1. Achterberg, "La banque dans la République Féderale Allemande", in *Institutions et mécanismes bancaires dans la C.E.E.*, p. 207f.

2. On the German banking system, cf. in particular Benoit, "Le système bancaire de l'Allemagne Fédérale", in *L'Allemagne d'aujourd'hui*, March-April 1957; Irmler, "Banking System of Western Germany", in *Banking Systems*, Columbia University Press, New York, 1959, p. 311-373; Mackenzie, *Banking Systems of Great Britain, France, Germany and the U.S.A.*, London, 1960; Association Fédérale des Banques Privées, *Le système bancaire dans la République Fédérale d'Allemagne*, Frankfurt am Main, 1962; Opie, "Western Germany", in *Banking in Western Europe*, Oxford University Press, London, 1962, p. 53-124; Rittershausen, "Banking in Western Germany", *Comparative banking*, Waterlow and Sons, London, 1963, p. 59f.; Kluge, "L'organisation bancaire dans la République Fédérale d'Allemagne", in *Revue de la Société d'Etudes et d'Expansion*, September-October 1967, p. 613f,; Muhlhaupt, *Strukturwandlungen im Westdeutschen Bankwesen*, Wiesbaden, 1971; Bundesverband Deutscher Banken, *The Banking System of the Federal Republic of Germany*, VIIth ed., September 1972; Peltzer and Ebendorf, *Banking in Germany*, Fritz Knapp Verlag, Frankfurt am Main, 1973; British Bankers' Association, *Prudential Regulations of Banks in the E.E.C.: Germany*, London, 1975.

3. Orsingher, *Les banques dans le monde*, p. 50f.

4. Cf. Janocha, "Money and credit policy of the Landesbanken and Girozentralen in the Federal Republic of Germany", in *Studi sulle politiche monetarie e creditizie per lo sviluppo economico*, pub. Cedam, Padua, 1970, p. 173f.

5. Cf. Samuelson, *La banque centrale de l'Allemagne de l'Ouest*, pub. Cujas, Paris, 1965; Arcucci, *La banca federale tedesca nell'economia della Germania occidentale*, pub. Giuffré, Milan, 1968.

6. Lange, *Die Unabhängigkeit der Deutsche Bundesbank*, pub. Universität von Mainz, 1966, p. 144f.; Schwarzer, "Die Notenbank muss noch unabhängiger werden", in *Junge Wirtschaft*, 1967, p. 380f.; Dessart, *Pour une Politique Monétaire Commune dans la CEE*, Brussels, 1971.

7. Cf. Deutsche Bundesbank, "Die Stellung der einzelnen Institut-gruppen im deutschen Banksystem", in *Monatsbericht der Deutsche Bundesbank*, March 1961.

8. Cf. Janocha, *op. cit.*, p. 174; Fries, *Die Girozentralen*, Stuttgart, 1959; Bartschat, *Die Geschäftspolitik der Girozentralen*, Hamburg, 1968.

9. Communautés Européennes, *La politique monétaire dans les pays de la C.E.E.*, Luxemburg, 1972, p. 99f.; in general cf. Jequier, *La politique des réserves obligatoires*, pub. Drotz, Geneva, 1966.

10. Cf. in particular Hubert, "Protection des dépôts bancaires en République Fédérale d'Allemagne", in *Banque*, September 1976, p. 845f.

11. Barmann, "Le secret bancaire en Allemagne Fédérale", in *Le secret bancaire dans la C.E.E. et en Suisse*, p. 15.

12. Achterberg, *op. cit.*, p. 253.

13. Barmann, *op. cit.*, p. 20f.

VII ITALY

1. GENERAL CONSIDERATIONS ON THE REGULATION OF CREDIT IN ITALY

The regulation of the banking sector is particularly well-developed in Italy. For the Italian legislator, banking activity is not the exclusive competence of the public authorities. Thus it does not have to be exercised by the Administration or by private institutions acting by virtue of a concession. Nevertheless it is "of public interest" and must therefore be subject to particular rules. This set of rules, whose basis is the Banking Act of 1936–1938, are very stringent and in fact certain authors have described the banking sector as a "highly collectivized" sector.[1]

In this respect, it should be noted that the Italian constitution, in art. 47, stipulates that "the Republic encourages and protects savings of all kinds; it disciplines, coordinates and controls the exercise of credit".

The direction and control of the banking sector is the responsibility of the Interministerial Committee for credit and savings (CICR), of the Treasury Minister and of the Bank of Italy which, being placed at the head of the banking sector, effectively assumes its direction. These bodies of direction, and in particular the Bank of Italy, are endowed with powers of control and of inspection, as well as very extensive disciplinary powers. They are thus used to taking administrative decisions of various natures, such as authorizations, instructions, orders, directives, etc. They are generally recognized to have the right to take measures of a general character to be imposed on all members of the banking sector.[2]

It should be added that in Italy at present, as a result of the fragmentary nature of the legislation and regulations, there is a kind of State monopoly of the exchange market. Recently, the Italian authorities have taken measures aimed at discouraging residents from investing outside Italy, and above all at putting a stop to the export of capital. These measures have caused some reduction in the resources at the disposal of the international capital market.

2. MONETARY POLICY AND CENTRAL BODIES; THE CENTRAL BANK

As far as the credit sector is concerned, the *Interministerial Committee for credit and savings* (CICR) is the body responsible for tracing out the broad lines of monetary, credit and exchange policy. The CICR was created by the decree of the provisional head of State no. 691 of 17 July 1947, to replace the old Committee of Ministers provided for by the Banking Act (Royal decree no. 375 of 12 March 1936) and suppressed in 1944. The Committee, in whose meetings the governor of the Bank of Italy participates by right and in fact very actively and often very decisively, is composed of the Treasury Minister, who presides over it, and the Ministers, of public works, of agriculture, of industry and trade, of foreign trade, of the budget and economic programming and of the Minister charged with State participations. The Banking Act stipulates that the Committee has recourse to the Bank of Italy for controls within its competence and in order to carry out its decisions. Within the frame-work of the directives issued by the Committee, which mark out general principles, the Bank of Italy plays a decisive role in choosing appropriate instruments and means to achieve the defined objectives; furthermore the governor of the Bank may take initiatives in order to facilitate the application of the measures decided on by the Committee.

The Bank of Italy (*Banca d'Italia*), which was created by Act no. 449 of 10 August 1893 and which is the only bank of issue since

1926 (Act no. 1362 of 25 May 1926) has undergone, as a result of the provisions of the banking act, important modifications which have transformed it from a joint-stock company, subject to the regulations of private law and authorized to carry out banking operations even with individuals, into an institution under public law whose activities are limited almost exclusively to relations with credit institutions. Its capital, divided into 300,000 nominal "shares" of 1,000 lira each, can only be held by savings banks, credit institutions under public law and banks of national interest, social security organizations and insurance companies.[3]

The Bank of Italy has its central office in Rome, 13 regional offices and 95 branches.

The *Higher Council* of the Bank, composed of 12 members nominated by the General Assembly with the approval of the President of the Republic, is charged with the nomination of the *Governor,* who enjoys complete freedom of action and full independence, the Director General and the Deputy Director General, still with the approval of the President of the Republic.

The Bank is subject to the control of the State, in consideration of the fact that it exercises functions of public interest and administers services on behalf of the State. This control is exercised by a permanent commission presided over by the Treasury Minister, which, on the request of the latter, expresses opinions on measures concerning bank notes, modifications made to the statute of the Bank and on the applications of laws concerning the bank of issue.

Apart from putting monetary policy into effect as indicated above, the Bank exercises control over all institutions, under public or private law, which collect savings from the public and distribute credit, whether in the short term (credit institutions) or in the medium and long term (specialized credit institutions).

In the exercise of the functions assigned to it by law, the Bank of Italy may require the institutions subject to its supervision to pass on balance sheets, periodic reports and any other useful information and may also carry out inspections of these establishments.

3. THE CREDIT INSTITUTIONS

All enterprises which collect savings from the public and devote themselves to credit operations, as well as specialized credit institutions (industrial, agricultural and land credit, construction credit, etc.) form part of the banking sector.

Italian banking law makes a distinction between short term (or ordinary) credit and medium and long term credit. Medium and long term credit is distributed almost exclusively by institutions under public law. All the same, since the end of the Second World War a tendency towards the so-called "universal" kind of bank may be observed. In fact, in Italy as in Belgium, one of the banks' means for financing industrial and commercial enterprises is to grant short term credits which are constantly renewed, so as to transform short term resources (for example demand deposits) into medium and long term credits. The "transformation" may also take place by virtue of special provisions issued by the monetary authorities: thus, in 1973 the banks were obliged to transform a certain part of deposits collected into long term bonds, and particularly into bonds of the specialized credit institutions.

We have spoken of banking enterprises: in fact banking activity is typically carried out by entrepreneurs, but art. 1 of the Banking Act defines it as "of public interest".

According to the terms of the aforesaid act, the following are considered as credit institutions: credit institutions under public law (*Banca Nazionale del Lavoro, Monte dei Paschi di Siena, Istituto Bancario San Paolo di Torino, Banco di Sicilia, Banco di Napoli* and *Banco di Sardegna*); banks of national interest (*Banca Commerciale Italiana, Credito Italiano* and *Banco di Roma*); banks set up in the form of joint-stock companies or share-issuing limited partnerships; personal banking enterprises which existed before the Banking Act came into force, which prohibited the formation of new credit institutions in the legal form of individual enterprises; the popular banks; the branch offices of foreign banks; savings banks and pawn-brokers; rural and artisan credit banks. At the end of 1970 there were 1,179 credit institutions in Italy representing a total of 10,807 agencies. The classification of credit establishments adopted by the Banking Act, according to the legal categories to which they belong, has not till now produced such a clear differentiation on the practical level excepts as concerns savings banks and the central institutions of each category, whose activities are intended to give technical and financial assistance to the associated banks and to coordinate their actions so far as possible.

The institutional differences between savings banks and other banks are reflected in the different part taken by the two categories in the principal items of investment and of the resources of the banking system. The 90 savings banks account for 73% of medium and long term investments and only 12% of short term investments. As for the make-up of their resources, the savings banks are characterized by a net predominance of savings deposits over current accounts while with other banks the opposite is true.

The spezialized credit institutions operate in the sector of medium and long term credit which is mostly practised by institutions and organizations of a public character having their own status but placed under the control of the State to which they often owe the capital with which they are endowed. The collection of savings is generally made by issuing bonds and to a lesser extent in the form of period deposits and cash vouchers with a period of maturity of between 18 months and 5 years and also long term credits obtained abroad.

As seen above, one of the characteristics peculiar to Italian banking organization is the presence, side by side, of public and private enterprises. The public institutions act in the same way as the private enterprises, enter into competition with them and do not benefit from any special privilege, since otherwise the private banks would disappear and the collectivization of the banking sector would become total and definitive. A number of these private banks, particularly the most important, are, it is true, companies with public participation, i.e. companies of which a considerable proportion of capital belongs to the State. Thus the public sector, including companies with State participation, ad-

minister 90% of credit operations and banking investments and
the private sector only 10% which, for the importance of the public
sector in the distribution of credit, places Italy in the first rank
amongst the countries with mixed economy.

4. ACCESS TO THE BANKING PROFESSION

According to art. 28 of the Banking Act, the enterprises mentioned
in art. 5 may be neither set up, nor commence operations, nor
create a branch office abroad or establish an agency in Italy without obtaining previous authorization from the Bank of Italy,
which is endowed with discretionary powers to this end. As a
result, in order to open a bank, two authorizations are necessary:
one for the creation of an enterprise in one of the forms provided
for by article 5; the other at the start of operations, i.e. in order
actually to carry out credit operations.

The fact that access to the banking profession is not free as in
other countries but strictly controlled, justifies the expression
"sectional organization of credit".[4]

According to the terms of article 29 of the Banking Act, all
credit institutions must be entered in a list of credit institutions
held by the Bank of Italy.

The last paragraph of article 28 submits their statutes and the
provisions which complete or modify them to the approval of the
Bank of Italy.

5. MERGERS AND ACQUISITION OF PARTICIPATIONS

The merging of banking enterprises in Italy offers a particularly
interesting example of the interpenetration of private law with
public law. It should be noted first of all that, according to Italian
law, the merging of companies in general may take the form either
of a merger in the true sense or else of an absorption. In the first
case, two or more companies join together and disappear in order
to give birth to a new company; in the second case, one or more

companies are absorbed and disappear within another pre-existing company which preserves its legal status.

Italian law, unlike French law, does not expressly provide for the splitting up of companies. However a part of legal doctrine maintains that such splitting is possible, even in the absence of explicit texts. Naturally the merger or absorption must be decided by the assemblies of the companies concerned and is only possible following and as a result of these decisions.

The merging of credit institutions, although it depends in some respects on the provisions of the Civil Code on the merging of companies, does present some original features.

Thus, credit institutions, unlike other companies, may merge even if they are not "homogeneous". Merger is possible not only between credit institutions set up in the form of joint-stock companies, but also between cooperatives, credit institutions under public law and credit institutions of an individual character.

Furthermore, banking mergers must be authorized in each case by the competent administrative authority when they are not purely and simply decided by this authority; in this case the merger is forced. In this field, as for the setting up of credit institutions, the administrative authority disposes of extensive discretionary powers. However in most cases the authorities have preferred to intervene in a non-coercive way, attempting rather to persuade the enterprises concerned (moral persuasion).[5]

As for the acquisition of participations, according to articles 33 and 35, paragraph 2, of the Banking Act, it is subject to the agreement of the Bank of Italy. On this point, the Bank of Italy, which was previously very reluctant to give such authorization, has recently developed a more favourable attitude.

6. THE SUPERVISION AND CONTROL OF THE BANKING SECTOR

In Italy, all public and private enterprises forming part of the banking sector are subject to a special administrative code of regulations which strictly limit their freedom to contract and their right to make undertakings. As seen above, administrative decisions may operate at each of the most important stages in the life of a bank.

As for the principal means of intervention at the disposal of the bodies charged with the direction and control of the credit sector, it may be observed that:

(1) article 29 of the Banking Act provides for the entry of all credit institutions in a list of credit institutions held by the Bank of Italy;

(2) the last paragraph of article 28 submits their statutes and provisions completing or modifying them to the approval of the Bank of Italy;

(3) the first paragraph of article 31 orders the communication to the Bank of Italy of periodic reports, balance sheets and any other data considered necessary;

(4) according to the second paragraph of article 31, officials of the Bank of Italy are entitled to proceed to periodic or unforeseen inspections;

(5) articles 47 and 56 subject operations of merging and absorption between credit institutions to prior authorization from the Bank of Italy;

(6) by virtue of article 34, the authorities are empowered to order the closure of a credit establishment either in consequence of a negative balance or else to distribute the bank's agencies over the territory in a more satisfactory way;

(7) by virtue of articles 57 and following, in the case of cessation of payment, they organize a provisional administration or else proceed to an administrative winding-up which, for a bank, replaces legal winding-up;

(8) the directors and officials of credit institutions are liable, in case of negligence or omission of their duties, to civil, penal and special administrative sanctions;

(9) still by virtue of article 57, a bank may have its authorization to act withdrawn and thus be struck off the list of credit institutions.

It must be added that in Italy all banks, with the exclusion of rural and artisan credit banks, are subject to the obligation to deposit reserves with the Bank of Italy. In 1975, the regime of obligatory reserves was considerably modified and reinforced.

7. THE STOCK-EXCHANGE IN ITALY

The setting up of stock-exchanges in Italy goes back to Act no. 680 of 6 July 1862. A more organic system of regulations was established by Act no. 272 of 20 March 1913, "on commercial stock-exchanges, intermediaries and stock-exchange contracts", completed by the regulations approved by royal decree no. 1068 of 4 August 1913 and modified several times in details, until the new regulations of 1974–1975.

Unlike the Anglo-Saxon countries where the stock-exchange is an institution under private law, in Italy the stock-exchange is organized as an institution under public law: the intervention of the State is to be seen above all in the creation of the principal bodies and the determination of their authority, in the exercise of powers of supervision and in the attribution of a monopoly in the negotiation of shares to specially qualified intermediaries, i.e. the stock-brokers, whose title is protected, and whose function received a true public investiture by virtue of article 1 of Act. no. 222 of 7 March 1925.

The new legislation is founded on Act no. 216 of 7 June 1974 and on the decree of the President of the Republic no. 138 of 13 March 1975. The 1974 Act set up the National Commission for Companies and the Stock-Exchange (CONSOB), composed of a president and four members all nominated by decree of the President of the Republic passed by the Council of Ministers. The Commission is a body of public administration and it was modelled on the *Security Exchange Commission* (SEC) of the United States as well as the Commission for Stock-Exchange Operations of France (COB). The CONSOB has general authority concerning the organization and functioning of the stock exchanges, and particularly concerning the admission of stocks and shares to quotation.

As for the general situation of the Italian stock-exchanges, it must be recalled that Italy is the only country of the European Economic Community where shares, with few exceptions are compulsorily registered; this compulsory registration has had the effect of turning away family savings from investment in shares.

Amongst the chief causes of the impoverishment of the Italian stock market, one should also consider the nationalization of the electrical industry which led to the disappearance from quotation of a large number of securities specially favoured for family savings, and the outdated structure of the Italian Stock-Exchange, to which individual savers and institutional investors continue to deny their support, leaving unchanged its speculative nature.[6]

8. THE PROTECTION OF BANKING SECRECY

Although the legal doctrine and jurisprudence of Italy have never placed in doubt the existence of a general obligation to maintain banking secrecy, the problem of knowing the source of this obligation has been much discussed.

Recently, the provision of subsection I of article 10 of the Banking Act, according to which "all opinions, information or data concerning credit institutions subject to the control of the Bank of Italy are subject to professional secrecy even with respect to the public authorities" has been invoked as the legal foundation for banking secrecy.[7]

As for banking secrecy with respect to the legal authorities, it is generally admitted that secrecy has much more importance in civil than in penal cases, given the difference of interest held by the two kinds of trial.

As for banking secrecy with regard to the revenue authorities, one can not affirm that secrecy is absolute, since there are provisions, especially in the new revenue legislation, which authorize the revenue agents to intervene with banks, but only in special cases.

NOTES

1. The text of the banking act, coordinated and revised by the Italian Banking Association, is published in *La legge bancaria e le altre norme essenziali in materia creditizia*, Rome, pub. Bancaria, 1972. On the Italian banking system, see in particular Vignocchi, *Il servizio del credito nell'ordinamento pubblicistico italiano*, Milan, pub. Giuffré, 1968; Nigro, *Profili pubblicistici del credito*, Milan, pub. Giuffré, 1972; Gerbi, "Institutions et mécanismes bancaires en Italie", in *Institutions et mécanismes bancaires dans les pays de la CEE*, Paris, Dunod, 1969, p. 300f; Gerbi, "Banking System of Italy", in *Banking Systems*, edited by B. H. Beckhart, Columbia University Press, New York, 1959, p. 421-517; Ceriani, "The Commercial Banks and Financial Institutions in Italy", in *Banking in Western Europe*, edited by R. S. Sayers, Oxford University Press, London, 1962; Lutz, "The Central Bank and the System of Credit Control in Italy", *ibid.*, p. 124-174; Ruta, *Il sistema della legislazione bancaria*, IInd edition, Bancaria, Rome, 1975; Banco di Roma, *The Italian Banking System*, Rome, 1969.

2. Cf. Mastropasqua, "La réglementation du crédit et les fusions bancaires en Italie", *Banque*, October 1976, p. 970f.

3. Cf. Communautés Européennes, *La politique monétaire dans les pays de la CEE*, Luxemburg, 1972, p. 209f.

4. Cf. Mastropasqua, *Ibid.*, p. 970.

5. Cf. Mastropasqua, *La fusione delle aziende di credito*, pub. Bancaria, Rome, 1974; Mastropasqua, "Aspetti pubblicistici della fusione delle aziende di credito", *Annali dell'Istituto di diritto pubblico dell' Università di Roma*, pub. Cedam, Padua, 1976.

6. Cf. Sertoli, "L'incidence des formes des valeurs mobilières sur l'intégration des marchés européens de valeurs mobilières", in *L'intégration des marchés européens des valeurs mobilières*, Université internationale de Sciences Comparées, Luxemburg, 1971, p. 64.

7. Cf. Ruta, "Le secret bancaire en droit italien", in *Le secret bancaire dans la CEE et en Suisse*, P.U.F., Paris, 1974, p. 119.

VIII IRELAND

1. A SURVEY OF THE IRISH ECONOMY

In the Irish Republic, as in most European countries, industry has substantially outgrown the agricultural sector, and in recent years industrial expansion has been the mainspring of economic growth.

Much of the country's external trade is with the United Kingdom. The Irish pound and the pound sterling exchange at par and there is free movement of funds between Ireland and the United Kingdom. British currency is freely accepted in the Republic of Ireland, while Irish currency circulates readily in Northern Ireland.

The Irish economy is characterised by a large and rapidly expanding public sector, with public capital formation accounting for somewhat more than half of total investment.[1]

2. BASIC LAWS AND AMENDMENTS

The Central Bank Act of 1942 gave the Central Bank the role of regulating the banking system in the interest of the public at large, but the need for more formal control was answered by the 1971 legislation, which conferred extensive licensing and supervisory powers on the Central Bank. The Central Bank Act of 1971 amends and extends the Currency Act of 1927 and the Central Bank Acts of 1942 and 1964. The four Acts together form the basis of Irish currency and banking legislation, and may be supplemented by regulations made by the Minister of Finance and the Central Bank.[2]

3. THE CENTRAL BANK

The Central Bank of Ireland came into existence in 1943 as a result of the Central Bank Act of 1942, and took the place of the Currency Commission which had been set up under the Currency Act of 1927. The issuing function was transferred to the Central Bank on its formation.

The 1942 Act empowered the Central Bank to act as lender of last resort but the liquidity of the system was such that this power was not used until 1955. The Bank was also empowered to take deposits from banks.

The Exchequer account was formerly kept at the Bank of Ireland (one of the leading commercial banks, founded in 1783) but was transferred to the Central Bank under the 1971 Act, though some public accounts are still held with the Bank of Ireland.

The monetary policy function of the Central Bank is set out in section 6 of the Central Bank Act of 1942, which gave the Bank "the general function and duty of taking (within the limit of the powers for the time being vested in it by law) such steps as the Board may from time to time deem appropriate and advisable towards safeguarding the integrity of the currency and ensuring that, in what pertains to the control of credit, the constant and predominant aim shall be the welfare of the people as a whole".

This statement of the general function and duty of the Bank is followed in the Act by a subsection empowering the Minister of Finance, whenever he thinks proper, to require the Governor of the Bank or the Board "to consult and advise with him in regard to the execution and performance by the Bank of the general function and duty imposed on the Bank".

The Central Bank Acts of 1942 and 1971 in effect give the Central Bank a large measure of autonomy.

Under the 1971 Act the Central Bank was made the licensing authority for banks, and formal powers were given to the Bank to require a holder of a banker's licence to maintain a specified ratio between assets and liabilities. These powers strengthened the position of the Bank particularly by providing an alternative instrument of monetary control in addition to those of moral suasion and quantitative guidelines formerly employed by it.

4. THE PRINCIPAL CREDIT INSTITUTIONS AND THEIR CHARACTERISTICS

All banks and other bodies engaged in "banking business" must be licensed and must also maintain a deposit in the Central Bank of Ireland in accordance with section 13 of the Central Bank Act of 1971. "Banking business" is defined by section 2 of the Act as: (a) the business of accepting deposits payable on demand or on notice or at a fixed or determinable future date, or (b) the business aforesaid and any other business normally carried on by a bank.

The main commercial banks in the Republic of Ireland, known as the associated banks, were founded in the late eighteenth and nineteenth centuries. The associated banks are the most important category of banks in the Republic of Ireland. The term "associated" comes from the Central Bank Act of 1942, which gave them a special relationship with the Central Bank. The major proportion of total monetary transactions in the economy is settled by cheques drawn on the associated banks. They operate a comprehensive current and deposit-account service, account for some 70% of total credit extended within the State by all banks and have an extensive branch network, with some 750 branches throughout the Republic of Ireland.

In 1965 and in 1966, the associated banks were the object of a series of regroupings that led to the birth of the Bank of Ireland Group and the Allied Irish Banks.

Banks other than the associated banks are classified as non-associated banks. The non-associated banks engage in commercial banking, in merchant banking and in consumer finance. They consist of subsidiaries of the associated banks, branches of North American banks, subsidiaries and affiliates of British banks and a number of other Irish banks together with two banks from other EEC countries.

For statistical purposes the non-associated banks are categorised under four broad groups. Six merchant banks constitute the first broad group, four of them being subsidiaries either of associated banks or of foreign banks.

The second broad group of non-associated banks consists of five North American banks, one of which is a joint venture with a domestically-controlled bank group.

The third category consists of eleven industrial banks whose business is mainly instalment credit.

The fourth category consists of a miscellaneous group of 16 banks, including two banks from other EEC countries.

5. LICENSING AND AUTHORIZATION

Under the Central Bank Act of 1971, a licence is required before starting banking business. The Central Bank now has discretionary power to grant a licence to any applicant, but may not refuse a licence without the consent of the Minister for Finance. The Central Bank may impose such conditions when granting a licence as it feels will promote the "orderly and proper regulation of banking". Similarly, the conditions of a licence may be amended, revoked or added to, and conditions may be imposed in relation to a licence from time to time by the Bank for the same object.

An applicant for a new banking licence must be a company, with minimum capital £ 1 million, so that a new one-man bank cannot be established.

6. EQUITY PARTICIPATIONS AND MERGERS

There are some limitations on participations in non-credit institutions. Permission is needed to hold more than 20% of another company's shares; the aggregate of all investments in the voting shares of other companies shall not exceed 30% of a bank's risk assets.

There are no statory provisions regulating bank mergers and changes of ownership, but the monitoring of participations in banks operates effectively as a merger control.

Any one shareholder, or what is deemed by the Central Bank to be an associated group of shareholders, shall not hold more than 20% of the shares of any class in a bank without the written consent of the Central Bank.[3]

7. THE SUPERVISION OF THE BANKING SYSTEM

The Central Bank is the lender of last resort and thus the main direct source of liquidity for the banks. Rediscounting by the Bank must be seen in the context of this function. Legislation relating to the provision of Central Bank credit is set out in section 7 of the Central Bank Act of 1942. Access to Central Bank credit is in all circumstances a privilege, and the Bank retains discretion to grant or refuse a request for rediscounting even if all the legal requirements as regards eligibility of bills are fulfilled.

In general, credit control has been one of the principal tools used in Ireland and the method of implementing credit control has developed fairly rapidly over the past decade.

The introduction of liquidity ratios for licensed banks towards the end of 1972 is of great importance from the point of view of monetary policy. There are two ratios, primary and secondary; the primary ratio relates to cash and deposits with the Central Bank, while the secondary ratio relates to government paper, e.g. Exchequer bills and government stock.

In addition to controlling the growth in monetary aggregates the Central Bank attemps to influence the purposes for which credit is used (selective control of domestic credit).

8. CREDIT INSTITUTIONS EXCLUDED FROM THE LICENSING AND SUPERVISION PROCEDURES

While the regulatory provisions apply to all associated and non-associated banks, the following credit institutions are excluded from the licensing and supervision procedures:

(a) *Building Societies.* – The building societies are an important part of the financial sector. They are the largest single providers of mortgage finance for housing in Ireland, providing some 70% of such finance.

(b) *The Post Office Savings Bank and Trustee Savings Bank.* – The Post Office Savings Bank and the five savings bank are not counted as a part of the banking system, although their liabilities are "near money". The savings banks have some 1,400 branches throughout the country.

(c) *Credit Unions.* – The growth of the credit union movement in Ireland since the movement's inception in the late 'fifties has been very rapid.

(d) *The Agricultural Credit Corporation Limited and the Industrial Credit Company Limited.* – Both the Agricultural Credit Corporation and the Industrial Credit Company were established by the State. The Agricultural Credit Corporation provides capital for financing agricultural development; its liabilities consist of deposits from the public, funds supplied by the Exchequer and the balance being provided by borrowing abroad. The Industrial Credit Company operates as an industrial development bank and provides capital for industry by medium- and long-term loans, direct share investment, industrial hire purchase and leasing facilities.

(e) *Friendly Societies.*

(f) *Investment Trust Companies.*

NOTES

1. European Communities, *Monetary policy in the countries of the EEC*, Brussels, 1974; Hein, "Under Two Flags—A Guide to Banking in Ireland", in *The Canadian Banker*, Spring 1968, p. 48-57.

2. British Bankers' Association, *Prudential Regulation of Credit Institutions in Ireland*, London, 1975.

3. British Bankers' Association, *op. cit.*

IX DENMARK

1. MONETARY POLICY AND CENTRAL BODIES; THE CENTRAL BANK

It is the responsibility of Danmarks Nationalbank, as the Central Bank of Denmark, to maintain a sound monetary system and to facilitate and regulate money transactions and lending activities (Danmarks Nationalbank Act of 7 April 1936). The Nationalbank is thus the central monetary authority of Denmark.

The Bank discharges its responsibilities in co-operation with the government, notably the Royal Bank Commissioners (at the present time: the Minister of Economic Affairs and the Budget) who supervises the performance of the duties assigned to the Bank under the Danmarks Nationalbank Act.[1]

The basic statutes governing the banking system are the Bank Act of 1930 and the Danmarks Nationalbank Act of 1936.

The Nationalbank enjoys the sole right of note issue. The Bank holds the government account and provides short-term finance when necessary. The above mentioned Danmarks Nationalbank Act of 7 April 1936 changed the status of the Bank from that of a joint-stock company to a self-governing non-profit institution.

The Bank is managed by a board of directors, a committee of directors and a board of governors. The Nationalbank is also the registration authority for commercial banks and savings banks, and has the usual central banking responsibilities in relation to them.[2]

2. THE PRINCIPAL CREDIT INSTITUTIONS AND THEIR CHARACTERISTICS

In the Danish banking system, commercial banks are distinguished from savings banks. Commercial bank and savings bank activities are governed by respectively the Commercial Bank Act of 15 June 1956 and the Savings Bank Act of 15 January 1960.

Under the terms of the Commercial Bank Act of 1956 a bank must be constituted in accordance with the provisions of the Companies Act. Only commercial banks are allowed to engage in banking business and they have the sole right to use the word "bank" in their names.

Under the terms of the Savings Bank Act of 1960 savings banks must be constituted as non-profit self-governing institutions whose profits may be allocated only to reserves or to activities serving public interests. The objects of savings banks are to accept interest-paying deposits from the general public and to invest such deposits in a safe manner. Only institutions complying with the provisions of the Savings Bank Act are entitled to use the designation "savings bank" in their names.

According to the Banking Act of 1930, supervision of the banks is exercised by the Government Inspector of Commercial Banks and Savings Banks, who is responsible to the Minister of Commerce.

In 1975, this Act was replaced by a new Act, i.e. Act n° 199 of 2 April 1974. According to paragraph 1, subsection 4 of the new law, commercial banks and savings banks are not authorized to operate outside the banking sector. As a rule, in order to avoid the possibility that banks exercise control over other enterprises by means of shares or participations, it is forbidden for banks to acquire majority participations in other enterprises (principle of banking specialization). However, shares in finance companies operating in the field of leasing and factoring are considered as admissible, as well as financial interest in companies providing services (for example data processing) for banks. Furthermore, the administrators of banks may not occupy important positions in other sectors of the economy.

According to paragraph 24, subsection 1 of the new act, for reasons of liquidity banks may not acquire or accept as guarantee for credits shares in a single company whose book value exceeds 15% of the bank's own capital. The same provision lays down that shares in the possession of a bank may not amount to more than 50% of own capital. The total holding, i.e. including credits of all kinds, in relation to a single client is only allowed within the limit of 35% of own capital. However, according to paragraph 23, subsection 1, in certain cases it is possible to enlarge the holding to 50%.

The Danish commercial banks are organised in the Federation of Danish Banks which acts as their representative in matters of common interest, as for example in discussion with the Central Bank in the formulation of monetary policy.

There has been a tendency towards increased concentration both in banks and savings banks. Between 1961 and 1971 the number of banks fell from 159 to 79, and that of savings banks from 477 to 371. The decline in the number of banks came partly from take-overs of small banks by medium-sized ones and partly by mergers among the small banks.[3]

3. OTHER FINANCIAL INSTITUTIONS

Amongst the most important specialized banks may be mentioned the *Denmark's Ship Credit Fund,* which was established in 1961 as a self-governing non-profit institution by Danmarks Nationalbank, commercial banks, insurance companies, shipyards and shipowners; the *Industrial Finance Institute,* which was established in 1958 by Danmarks Nationalbank, commercial banks, savings banks, insurance companies and the Federation of Danish Industries; the *Municipal Credit Institute,* which makes credit available to local government authorities, joint municipal undertakings, district heating stations, etc.

Furthermore there are the *mortgage credit institutions* whose activities are regulated by the Mortgage Credit Act of 10 June 1970.

Apart from the Post Giro, which is a government agency managed by the PTT Administration, there are no other governmental banking institutions in Denmark.

4. SUPERVISORY SYSTEM

In Denmark there is no pre-entry licence, but anyone carrying out banking activities is controlled by the Government Inspector of Commercial Banks and Savings Banks.

It is the duty of the Government Inspector to undertake regular examination of the methods of operation and the financial position of all commercial and savings banks. His decisions may be appealed to the Ministry of Commerce. He also promulgates rules on the form of presentation of monthly balance sheets, annual accounts, etc., of commercial and savings banks.

In addition, the Government Inspector is the monopoly control authority in fields where the Monopoly Control Act applies to commercial and savings banks.

There are no legal reserve requirements for commercial banks, but in 1965 the Nationalbank assumed, by agreement with the banks, the power of requiring them to make deposits with itself.

NOTES

1. Cf. European Communities, *Monetary Policy in the Countries of EEC*, supplement 1974, Brussels.

2. Cf. Morgan, Harrington & Zis, *Banking Systems and Monetary Policy in the EEC Countries*, London, 1974, p. 17.

3. Morgan, Harrington & Zis, *op. cit.*, p. 18.

X COMPARATIVE ASPECTS AND PROSPECTS FOR THE EVOLUTION OF THE BANKING SECTOR

1. RELATIONS BETWEEN GOVERNMENTS AND CENTRAL BANKS

Monetary policy represents one of the major functions of the state and yet, unlike defence, foreign relations or public works, the monetary power, in almost all countries, is exercised by the central banks, which represent separate and distinct entities from the single governments and enjoy a considerable degree of freedom or autonomy.[1]

However, in all countries the central banks, although formally they enjoy full independence, work in close collaboration with the governments.

The central bank has an important responsibility to encourage the development of an efficient and flexible financial system to serve the needs of the economy as a whole as well as the special requirements of the policy makers. Normally some measure of independence will encourage a central bank to develop the vigour and freshness of approach, the technical competence and flexibility, and the basic understanding of market forces and attitudes needed to discharge these functions effectively.

Since the central bank has a special relationship with the markets in which it is at once an operator and to some extent a controller, these operations impose upon it a form of internal organization which is much closer to that of a business enterprise than that of a department of the civil service.[2]

No central bank is headed by a cabinet member, but in many cases governors and directors of central banks, when their term of office has finished, have been called to take on important governmental responsibilities.

To sum up, in all countries of the Western world, monetary power tends to be regarded more and more as an autonomous power, separate from the other functions of the state, and this is partly due to the great prestige enjoyed by its exponents. "Good monetary policy is above all else a matter of men; good policy requires men of ability, perception, and sound judgment, regardless of where they may be located in the governmental hierarchy. Central banking is not something which can be learned in a few weeks or a few months. Good central bankers must be career men, not subject to the vicissitudes of political successes and defeats ... They must be given powers and responsibilities commensurate with the importance of the work they are asked to do".[3]

2. NATIONALIZATION OF THE BANKING SECTOR

After the wave of nationalizations of central banks which occurred in the post-war period (Bank of France in 1945, Bank of England in 1946, Central Bank of Holland in 1948), although new nationalizations have occasionally been proposed, it cannot at present be affirmed that there is a tendency towards nationalization of the banking sector within the countries of the EEC.

As for the nationalization of central banks (which in no way may be considered as simple private enterprises, being responsible since the end of the first world war for public functions of exceptional importance), this phenomenon has involved the more ancient institutions, while the central banks of more recent formation have maintained their original form, so as to avoid structural changes in a relatively short interval of time, which changes could have obstructed the process of consolidation and reinforcement of their role within the banking system. Moreover, in all countries the central banks work in close collaboration with the governments whatever their legal character. For this reason, the nationalization of the central banks of France, England and Holland as well as the semi-nationalization of that of Belgium did not entail any substantial change in their way of working.

As for the nationalization of banks in the private sector, it may be observed that, while the intervention of the state in this sector has been seen to some extent in all countries, this intervention (with the exception of the nationalization of the large deposit banks in France in 1945) has not been made through the nationalization of banks, but rather through the creation of new public institutions, specializing in certain branches of credit (as for example the financing of foreign trade, credit for local communities, etc.), and other instruments for public intervention in the economy.

Moreover, while on the one hand it must be admitted that banks have to be subject to a special legal regime to conform with the aims of economic and monetary policy, on the other hand it does not appear that the banking sector is the sector which best lends itself to nationalization, since it is not a field dominated by bureaucratism and routine operations, but a field in which competitiveness, individual initiative and personalized relations are all-important.

Furthermore, it must not be forgotten that the transition from private property to public property in practice is almost always an irreversible process.

Lastly, any nationalization can influence the government concerned in the direction of self-sufficiency, in open contradiction to the community spirit and European economic unification.

3. DESPECIALIZATION OF THE BANKING SECTOR

As for the organization of the private banking sector, in all the EEC countries there are on the one hand the large credit institutions (commercial banks, deposit banks or clearing banks, set up in the form of joint-stock companies) and on the other hand the specialized banks, i.e. the investment banks, the financial institutions, the *banques d'affaires* (France), the merchant banks (England). However, while within each sector a certain tendency to extend the range of services offered to the public may be noted, one may also note a diminishing of the existing differences between the various categories of financial intermediaries. This phenomenon is particularly noticeable for commercial banks and savings banks but also affects merchant banks.

It must be added that while in Italy the banking system plays a dominant role on the financial market, in Great Britain, Germany and Holland the banks work in conjunction with other financial operators.

In Germany, Holland and Luxemburg the banks have a more distinctly "universal" character, while the principle of specialization, understood both as the separation between short term credit and medium and long term credit and as the ban on acquisition of participations and territorial specialization, is particularly rigid in Belgium and above all in Italy.

4. BANKING CONCENTRATION

In all the countries taken into consideration (with the exception of Luxemburg, which moreover has a financial market in full expansion) one may notice a marked tendency towards banking concentration, above all on the initiative of the large commercial banks.

In most European countries, banking concentration is historically linked with industrial concentration, in the sense that the gradual expansion of industry forced the banks to increase their dimensions so as to maintain their independence with respect to the industrial enterprises. Furthermore, since the large enterprises which arose from industrial concentration continued, and even now continue, to have recourse to banking credit, it was necessary to maintain a certain equilibrium between the wealth of the debtor and that of the creditor.

In fact, banking concentration facilitates the financing of costly research programmes exceeding the possibilities of isolated and small scale credit institutions; it facilitates the use of more advanced techniques (electrical accounting machines, data processing centres etc.); it allows considerable economies to be made in general expenditure and reduces the banks' need for liquidity.

Furthermore, banking concentration lets savers develop greater trust with regard to the banks which for their part may set up a network of agencies and branches which is more rational and more suited to local needs, at the same time eliminating superfluous enterprises.

Amongst the various forms of banking concentration, the merger, which carries out total and definitive integration both at the economic level and at the legal level, is that which best meets the objectives of the policy of banking concentration.[4]

The most spectacular banking mergers have been those in Holland in 1964, in Belgium in 1965, in France in 1966 and in England in 1968.

As for the degree of concentration and its effects on the collection of deposits, it is interesting to note that at the end of 1975 the London "big four" collected 75% of deposits, while the two most important banks in Holland and Belgium collected, respectively, 35% and 32% of deposits.

5. THE INTERNATIONALIZATION OF THE BANKING SECTOR

In recent experience, there has also been a marked tendency for banks to carry out their activities on an international scale: thus one may see the formation of multinational banks created on the initiative of banks and financial institutions of various nationalities, in the same way as has already taken place for multinational companies. On the other hand, the internationalization of the banking sector goes hand in hand with that of the industrial sector because of the close interdependence which exists between industry and the banks.

The process of internationalization is still in progress on account of the continuous growth of the international capital market; at the community level it can however favour the harmonization of the banking systems of the countries of the EEC.

On this subject it should be remembered that the Treaty of Rome which set up the European Economic Community affirmed amongst other things the principle of free circulation of capital within the Community. In respect of this principle the action of the authorities charged with the monetary policy of each country should not obstruct the movement of capital between one country and another with authoritarian measures (which in any case have shown themselves incapable of preventing the flight of capital from certain countries), but should rather tend to protect savings ensuring better conditions for their just remuneration, and in the same way, austerity plans intended to combat inflation should not entail new restrictions nor discourage the international circulation of capital.

6. TRANSFORMATION OF BANKING RESOURCES

On a more technical level, a growing tendency may be noted, even though this varies from country to country, towards a lengthening in the duration of credits granted to enterprises, with a particular increase in medium term credits: this is the phenomenon of the so-called "transformation" of banking resources, i.e. the transformation of a part of the short term resources (for example demand deposits) into long and medium term credit.[5]

There is no doubt, however, that beyond a certain point the banks may not take upon themselves the risk of transformation, lending, in the medium and long term, resources of short duration, since this could compromise their liquidity and solvency. In this respect it is as well to remember that the crisis of the English secondary banks, which arose towards the end of 1973, was chiefly caused by the fact that these banks had made too many long term investments using funds received in the short term since their own funds were insufficient.

7. CONDITIONS FOR ACCESS AND SUPERVISION OF THE BANKING SECTOR

As far as access to the banking sector and the opening of agencies is concerned, it must be underlined that they are rigidly controlled in Italy where the discretionary authorization of the Bank of Italy is necessary both for the creation of a new bank and for the opening of agencies and branches, while in France and in Ireland some degree of liberalization may be noted. In England and in Holland access is in practice free and the reforms which are about to be introduced cannot radically change the existing situation.

As regards in particular the conditions for access and the controls existing in the various countries, it should be remembered that in all these countries a system of prior authorization for the exercise of banking activities is already in force or is about to be introduced. In this respect the accent is placed on the conditions of respectability and professional qualification, which at least on the moral level establish a guarantee for depositors, and also on a given minimum capital.

In the same way, in all these countries there exists or there is about to be introduced a form of legal protection of the terms "bank", "banker", etc.; this is justified by the fact that the exercise of the banking profession, in the general opinion, takes on a particular character of public concern since the banking sector is closely linked to the fulfilment of the economic and social policy of the governments.

Although in some countries banks may be set up in the form of individual enterprises (Holland, Great Britian), there is nevertheless a preference in all countries of the EEG for banks set up in the form of joint-stock companies.

As for the kind of preventive controls, it should be specified that in Denmark, in Ireland and above all in Germany these controls are objective and not discretionary, in the sense that the authorities only have to ensure the observance by the banks of the conditions of admissibility prescribed directly by law.

When talking of controls over the banking sector, the first

distinction that should be made is that between controls applied to credit institutions with the aims of preserving their viability as going concerns, and of protecting the interests of their depositors, and the monetary or credit controls which are imposed for economic management motives. However it is not always easy to distinguish the former from the latter, since there may be a kind of control which satisfies at the same time both the need for solvency and protection of depositors and the needs of monetary policy. Thus for example the control exercized by the central banks through the imposition of obligatory reserves is not only a means to guarantee the solvency and liquidity of the banks but may also act as a kind of "sterilization" of bank deposits.

As for the supervision of the banking sector in different countries, in general there is a preference for the practices based on the principles of gentlemen's agreement and moral persuasion (England, Holland, Luxemburg), and for that of "mutual consent" based on periodic and systematic exchange of viewpoints between the central bank and the banking and financial institutions (Belgium). These practices allow amongst other things the realization of a kind of self-discipline within the sector.

In any case it may be observed that the country with the fewest explicit regulations is the United Kingdom, while the most strictly regulated country is Italy.

Moreover, it may be observed that where there has been a recent banking reform, the powers of the supervisory authorities have been extended and reinforced. This is because these reforms were influenced by the crisis which struck the western world particularly hard and which clearly obstructed the process, of its nature slow and difficult, of economic and monetary union between the countries of the EEC, also provoking dangerous tendencies towards economic nationalism. It is not by chance that the most important reforms have been seen in the countries with the most liberal tradition with regard to the banking sector (Great Britain, Holland, Germany), while in the countries where there was already a fairly well-developed control system (France, Italy) the crisis has not up to now provoked any tendency towards reform of the banking legislation presently in force.

On a more technical level, a general tendency may be noted towards the imposition of obligatory reserves and the fixing of liquidity and solvency ratios.

Other projects presently under study, following the example of the USA, provide for the introduction of a system of compulsory deposit insurance up to a given amount. This system of insurance is already provided for by the new Dutch banking law, although the amount has not yet been fixed, while the bill presented by the British government provides for the creation of a depositors' protection fund for all deposits entrusted to institutions recognized as banks up to a value of 10,000 pounds. Lastly, in Germany the system of deposit guarantee was set up by the banks themselves on a voluntary basis. At first sight it might seem a paradox that the system of deposit insurance is considered necessary in the very countries in which the freedom of the banking sector is greater and public control less: thus in Holland, Great Britain and Germany it is in the process of being introduced while there is no such plan in Italy, France or Belgium. The fact is that in the latter countries, the intensity and the range of public controls was considered sufficient in itself to ensure the stability and solvency of the banking sector as a whole, while in the other countries the greater flexibility of the control system makes it necessary to adopt measures which ensure an adequate protection for depositors in case of crisis.

8. TRENDS IN THE STOCK-EXCHANGE

The stock-exchange in Europe is characterized by the great difference in organization in the various countries: thus for example there are stock-exchanges organized in the form of private associations over which there is no State control (Great Britain), while there are also stock-exchanges organized as public institutions and controlled directly or indirectly by the State (France and Italy); furthermore, the banks may dominate the market in stocks and shares (Germany), share it with the stock-brokers (Holland), or else have no direct relationship with the stock-exchange (Great Britain); lastly there is only one country in which foreign issues are authorized (Germany).

In any case, as far as control over the stock-exchange is concerned an evolution may be observed towards forms of control which answer the actual needs of the market in stocks and shares more effectively, through the creation of special bodies which, though linked with the public administration, are outside the bureaucratic apparatus of the State and possess all the powers necessary for a complete supervision and regulation of the market.

As for the evolution towards new forms of exercise of intermediary activities on the stock-exchange on the other hand, the most typical aspect of this evolution is the creation of brokerage companies following the example of Japan since 1948. This evolution, which has been proceeding for some time in the USA and Great Britain may now be seen in France and Belgium. Because of the advantages which it entails when compared with the exercise of intermediary activities by individuals, it is easy to predict that the forming of specialized brokerage companies will represent the principal element in the new organization of the stock-exchange for all the European countries.

9. FURTHER PROSPECTS FOR THE EVOLUTION OF THE BANKING SECTOR

In the previous pages, we have already examined some of the tendencies in the development of the banking and stock-exchange sectors, for example the despecialization and internationalization of the banking sector and the transformation of banking resources.

Further prospects are offered by the gradual evolution of the banking world towards new forms of activity both at the national and at the international level.

Two aspects in particular should be mentioned here, i.e. the diversification of the services offered to clients and the development of new forms of inter-bank cooperation.

As for the diversification of services offered to clients, this occurs both through traditional operations and also through a new range of banking services, amongst which should be mentioned consumer credit, mortgage credit, underwriting, leasing and factoring.[6] Both leasing and factoring may either be carried out directly or through affiliated holding companies.

The management of clients' portfolios, which in the past was carried out by banks exclusively on behalf of richer clients, is now in many cases carried out on behalf of all clients who wish to make use of this service, independently of their economic situation.

The application of the techniques of information theory to banking procedures and operations will allow the traditional operations to be carried out in a much more rapid and effective way and make new operations possible.

As for the development of new forms of cooperation, a distinction may be made between operative and institutional cooperation. The first is more limited and is directed towards the carrying out of particular operations, for example the setting up of trusts for the issue of Euro-bonds and the granting of Euro-credits. The second may take on the form of agreements to collaborate (clubs), which are gradually replacing the old matching agreements between banks and in which the participating banks maintain full autonomy of administration (eg. EBIC, Europartners), or else the form of bank consortia.

10. HARMONIZATION OF BANKING LEGISLATION AND LIBERALIZATION OF BANKING ACTIVITIES WITHIN THE *EEC*

The objective of the Treaty of Rome was, amongst other things, to create a zone in which not only persons, goods and services but also capital could circulate freely. The latter aim has not so far been achieved and is still far from being achieved. In fact, with the aim of making article 67 of the Treaty of Rome effective, the European Community adopted a certain number of directives in the years between 1960 and 1965 whose purpose was to eliminate all restrictions to the free circulation of capital. But the time was not yet ripe: so many amendments and so many reservations were brought forward by the various governments over these directives that they became practically inoperative. In fact, all the governments declared themselves in favour, in principle, of the affirmation and widening of the freedom of circulation of capital, and also of full freedom for international transactions, but in practice almost all put up obstacles, pointing to problems and difficulties in the balance of payments, the flight of capital (Italy) or the protection of the national market. The greatest obstacles to European integration were, and still are, national protectionism, currency and capital movement restrictions, concern about inflation, discriminatory taxation and barriers to transnational access by financial institutions and intermediaries to markets abroad.

Another obstacle to banking integration, in our modest opinion, is created by the attitude of government authorities and central banks in the various countries: especially in those countries in which legislative and administrative regulation of the banking sector is very detailed (France, Belgium) and the powers of the central bank are particularly extensive (Italy) the central banks are led to exercise their supervision over the banking sector in a "paternalistic" and "protectionist" manner and are jealous of their powers. Perhaps they are afraid that the harmonization of banking legislation could lead to the loss of some of their powers and hence of their authority.

For this reason, in official discussions, following declarations in favour of harmonization and banking integration in general, there are always objections and reserves on more specific subjects, i.e. at the point when these declarations should pass into operation. Amongst the most frequent objections is that it is not possible to apply the same disciplinary code to different and very heterogeneous systems; and that each country is confronted with particular problems that require different solutions.

However, although this kind of idea may on the one hand ensure a more "personalized" disciplinary code which conforms better to the needs of each country, on the other hand it is an "immobile" solution and is without doubt an obstacle to European integration.

Only the conscious renunciation by the authorities and central banks of each country of a whole series of particular powers and instruments will allow European integration of the banking sector to make some steps forward.

One step forward was achieved with the liberalization directive of June 28, 1973,[7] in which discriminatory treatment of the establishments of financial institutions from other Member States or of the rendering of services by these institutions in another Member State without their being established there is prohibited.[8]

Furthermore, since the problem of the credit institutions' freedom of establishment and of their freedom to offer services is closely connected with that of eliminating differences in legislation between Member States, with particular reference to admission to banking activity, on 12 December 1974 the Commission of the European Communities presented a draft directive relating to the coordination of provisions of law, of regulation and of administration concerning admission to carry out activities for credit institutions and their execise of such activities.[9] This draft directive requires for the establishment of a new bank an authorization either of the central bank or the state authority. This authorization will in future be subject to certain objective conditions, e.g. minimum amount of capital, conditions of professional qualification and respectability of directors, etc., so that the power to grant authorization is not referred to a discretional decision of the competent authority.

NOTES

1. Cf. Kriz, "Central Banks and the State Today", *American Economic Review*, September 1948, p. 576f.; Frère, "Economic Growth and Monetary Stability", *International Financial News Survey*, November 1964, p. 422f; Ratchford, "The Government and the Central Bank in a Free Society", in *Economic Systems and Public Policy: Essays in honor of*

Calvin Bryce Hoover, Duke University Press, Durham, N.C., 1966, p. 6of.

2. Cf. *Report of the Committee on the Working of the Monetary System (Radcliffe Committee)*, Cmnd. 827, London, 1959, p. 274.

3. Cf. Ratchford, *op. cit.*, p. 81.

4. Cf. Mastropasqua, *La fusione delle aziende di credito*, Rome, 1974, in particular sec. 1 of chapter 2.

5. The point of departure for the doctrine of "transformation" is to be found in the work of two American economists, Gurley & Shaw, *Money in a Theory of Finance*, where the idea is expressed that any financial intermediary, whether from the banking sector or not, is essentially a "transformer" of credits.

6. "Factoring" takes its origin from the practice of invoice guaranteed financing: the applicant sends invoices to be paid by his clients as collateral guarantee for a loan and pays off his debt at the same time as he redeems his money. This technique was well known and widespread in the USA in the thirties and a variation of it was in fact called "factoring": the manufacturer or wholesale trader, finding it financially impossible to guarantee the accounts of his own clients sells them to the factor who then redeems them for the sums owing. These operations were generally carried out by holding companies, while the banks were reluctant to undertake them. In fact it is clear that such operations are particularly costly and complex, since they require an enormous amount of investigation and inspection both of the borrower and of his clients.

7. Official Journal of the European Communities, n° L-194, July 16, 1973.

8. Cf. Gavalda, "La libération de l'établissement et des prestations des services bancaires dans la CEE", in *Revue trimestrielle de droit européen*, 1974, p. 695f.; Campet, "La libération de l'activité bancaire dans la CEE", in *Banque*, 1974, p. 259f.; Détienne, "La liberté d'établissement des banques et des autres établissements financiers", in *Revue de la Banque*, 1973, p. 424f.; Clarotti, "L'armonizzazione delle legislazioni bancarie alla luce degli ultimi avvenimenti", in *Credito Popolare*, 1975, p. 181f.

9. Official Journal of the European Communities, n° C-12, January 17, 1975.

INDEX OF AUTHORS